After work fast

quick roasts • fabulous salads • brilliant barbecues • easy pizzas

THE AUSTRALIAN
Women's Weekly

Contents

Like most of you, I've worked for years and gone home night after night fretting about what to make for dinner. Unlike most of you, I work with and around food all day, but don't think this gives me an advantage. In fact, just the opposite: I am OVER food when I leave the office, sated after the daily eight-hour assault on all my senses. Easy and quick are on my after-work menu, too, so this book can answer all our mealtime prayers, its clever yet accessible, basic but enticing recipes providing a welcome lifeline for the working warrior in need of inspiration.

Pamela Clark

Food Director

Home Truths

Yes, it is possible. You can come home from work and put together a great meal without stress, frenzy or multi-tasking meltdown. You'll even have time to change your clothes and sit down with a drink to watch the evening news: wonders *will* never cease. And the key to this marvellous miracle is simple: just a little pre-planning, organisation and imagination on your part. The best way to stymie enthusiasm for cooking is through routine and repetition: if you just keep churning out the same repertoire week after week, you'll lose interest and your family will too – and suddenly that quick fix known as takeaway can inveigle its way onto your table.

There are a few simplistic home truths to help counter both any ongoing relationship with fast foods and a lack of passion for cooking after work. First, we live in a country with a climate capable of producing an amazingly wide variety of produce virtually year round, accessible and affordable to everyone. Next, add to this bounty of fresh foods the luxuries afforded by life in a multi-cultural society: sample the ingredients typical of the various ethnic cuisines that have practically become native to us, and you can create a recipe list interesting enough and varied enough to stretch around the world.

Third, avoid panic by organising a well-stocked pantry of ready-to-use items such as tetra-paks of stock; packaged bread products such as pizza bases, chapatis and tortillas; pastas and rices; cans of tomatoes, beans, chickpeas, tuna and salmon; and bottled salad dressings, sauces, salsas, pastes and pestos. Keep frozen several individually wrapped bacon rashers, mince patties and cutlets (for quick thawing) as well as one or two different vegetables, plus always have cheese, eggs and butter in your refrigerator. Marry a list of meal ideas with the fresh items you buy on the way home and the staples ready and waiting in your kitchen, and let the celebration begin. It won't be long before you can make a pasta sauce by the time it takes the water to come to a boil, or a curry while the rice is steaming.

Don't be overly rigid with your concept of what an evening meal should be: there's nothing wrong with "breakfast" for dinner, like eggs with hash-browns or fritters, and a bowl of made-on-the-weekend soup with a BLT is possibly even more satisfying at night than midday. And don't be a snob when it comes to using convenience foods: they got their name with good reason, and their number and quality have grown rapidly and remarkably during the past decade. Making use of a jar of Thai green curry paste or a tub of fresh rocket and cashew pesto will dramatically reduce preparation times, and any taste difference between these and homemade is so negligible as to be impossible to discern.

Everything called for in this book can be found in your supermarket or at the local deli and greengrocer, and dinner can be on the table in around a half hour or less without sacrificing flavour or annihilating your peace of mind. And that's really the point, isn't it? We'd all like to unwind at home after work over a leisurely, angst-free meal that hasn't cost the earth in terms of labour or time. As you start cooking your way through this fantastic selection of recipes, you'll be surprised and delighted at how simple it can be to get an exciting evening meal on the table after work.

- Mix it up! Don't serve the same dishes week after week just because they're easy enough for you to make blindfolded.
- Start and keep updating a "Weeknight Meals" file with recipes, ideas and shortcuts.
- Keep plenty of tasty, exciting and versatile staple ingredients in the pantry and freezer that, when combined with one or two fresh items you pick up on your way home, will make preparation minimal.
- List your pantry and freezer contents, noting what you use up and/or replenish; that way, you'll never fall short and go into panic mode.
- Take advantage of the many shops that specialise in the foods of different nations to increase both your recipe repertoire and your exposure to new flavour sensations.
- Make use of your butcher's trimmed, marinated or crumbed meats and your supermarket's bags of washed salad leaves or pre-cut vegetables.
- Don't forget that the microwave oven is the busy cook's best friend: it can't do everything but it can steam vegetables and poach fish better and faster than any other kitchen tool.
- Think ahead: make soups, casseroles and curries on the weekend (refrigerate one night's dinner and freeze the rest in meal-size portions); marinate meat and poultry the night before.

Barbecue & Grill

rosemary

It's true that rosemary is for remembrance…and it's not hard to recollect food you've eaten that was imbued with its distinctively pungent lemon and pine flavour. Native throughout the southern Mediterranean, it's used in many stews and sauces in the French region of Provence and in northern Italy, and it's sprinkled over grilling kebabs and chops everywhere from France to Turkey. Its robust taste offers a foil to the richness of roast lamb, pork and game, and it's a lively addition to salad dressings. Mixed with lemon and garlic, it makes a perfect marinade for any meat that's to be grilled or barbecued, and whole stems can be whittled into skewers for souvlaki.

salmon fillets

Originally from the north Atlantic, this prized table fish has been farmed locally and sold throughout the country for more than 20 years. An oily fish, it's a rich source of the good omega-3 fatty acids that help protect against certain diseases. Its red-pink flesh and moist, delicate flavour make it an ideal meat to be grilled or barbecued; it's also good poached, pan-fried or eaten raw in sushi and sashimi. Most fillets and cutlets have had the bones removed when you buy salmon, so there'll be no time lost getting it ready for cooking. Salmon fillets, wrapped in foil with a few herbs and lemon juice, make a great quick grilled main course.

flat mushrooms

There are a vast number of mushrooms found in our greengrocers these days, and one of the best and certainly the most versatile of the cultivated variety is the flat mushroom (generally identified simply as "flats" – and, unfortunately, all too often as "field", which is misleading because the field is a wild mushroom that grows on forest floors and is seldom available commercially). Intensely earthy flavoured, large and dark, very dense and meaty in texture, flats are as good filled then barbecued and eaten as a main course as they are sliced thickly, quickly grilled with a little butter, a splash of balsamic and a sprinkle of herbs then strewn over bruschetta.

sumac

Ever since Middle-Eastern and Moroccan flavours began appearing on restaurant menus, we've tasted and fallen in love with the taste of sweet and sour sumac. A deep-purple-red astringent spice coarsely ground from berries growing on shrubs that flourish wild around the Mediterranean, sumac adds a tart, lemony flavour to dips and dressings and goes well with poultry, fish and meat. Mix sumac with olive oil and brush the mixture over a whole butterflied chicken on the grill for a luscious deep mahogany colour, or stir a teaspoon of sumac into a cup of plain greek-style yogurt and dollop it over a takeaway barbecued bird for flair and zing.

Spiced lamb burger with tzatziki

preparation time 20 minutes
cooking time 10 minutes
serves 4

Tzatziki is a Greek yogurt dip made with cucumber, garlic and sometimes chopped fresh mint. You can buy tzatziki ready-made in supermarkets and delis.

500g lamb mince
½ small red onion (50g), chopped finely
1 egg yolk
½ cup (35g) stale breadcrumbs
2 tablespoons sumac
1 large loaf turkish bread (430g)
250g tzatziki
350g watercress, trimmed
¼ cup (60ml) lemon juice
225g can sliced beetroot, drained

1 Combine lamb, onion, egg yolk, breadcrumbs and half the sumac in medium bowl; shape mixture into four patties.
2 Cook patties on heated oiled grill plate (or grill or barbecue) until cooked.
3 Meanwhile, preheat griller. Trim ends from bread; cut remaining bread into quarters then halve pieces horizontally. Toast, cut-sides up, under grill.
4 Combine remaining sumac and tzatziki in small bowl. Combine watercress and juice in another bowl.
5 Sandwich patties, tzatziki mixture, beetroot and watercress between bread pieces.

per serving 21.1g total fat (7.5g saturated fat); 2604kJ (623 cal); 60g carbohydrate; 43.8g protein; 8g fibre

Orange and soy salmon parcels

preparation time 10 minutes
cooking time 10 minutes
serves 4

4 x 200g salmon fillets
4 green onions, sliced thinly
1cm piece fresh ginger (5g), sliced thinly
2 cloves garlic, sliced thinly
¼ cup (60ml) light soy sauce
1 tablespoon finely grated orange rind
⅓ cup (80ml) orange juice
2 teaspoons grated palm sugar
450g baby buk choy, chopped coarsely
350g broccolini, halved crossways

1 Place each fillet on a piece of lightly oiled foil large enough to completely enclose fish. Combine onion, ginger, garlic, sauce, rind, juice and sugar in small jug; divide mixture among fish pieces. Gather corners of foil above fish; twist to enclose securely.
2 Cook parcels on heated oiled grill plate (or grill or barbecue) about 5 minutes or until fish is cooked as desired.
3 Meanwhile, boil, steam or microwave buk choy and broccolini, separately, until tender; drain. Serve salmon with vegetables.
per serving 14.8g total fat (3.2g saturated fat); 1471kJ (352 cal); 6.2g carbohydrate; 45.6g protein; 5.6g fibre

Sumac chicken with minted eggplant

preparation time 10 minutes
cooking time 15 minutes
serves 4

Tahini is a sesame seed paste available from
Middle Eastern food stores, many supermarkets and
health food stores. It is most often known as one of
the main ingredients in hummus and baba ghanoush.

1 teaspoon finely grated lemon rind
⅓ cup (80ml) lemon juice
2 teaspoons sumac
2 teaspoons caster sugar
1 tablespoon tahini
800g chicken tenderloins
2 medium eggplants (600g), sliced thickly
¼ cup (60ml) olive oil
½ cup coarsely chopped fresh mint
1 lemon (140g), sliced thickly

1 Combine rind, half the juice, sumac, sugar,
tahini and chicken in large bowl.
2 Cook chicken on heated oiled grill plate (or grill
or barbecue) until cooked. Remove from heat;
cover to keep warm.
3 Cook eggplant on cleaned heated oiled grill plate
until browned; combine eggplant in medium bowl
with remaining juice, oil and mint.
4 Serve chicken and eggplant with lemon.
per serving 28.3g total fat (5.7g saturated fat);
2107kJ (504 cal); 14.2g carbohydrate;
45.9g protein; 5.1g fibre

Balsamic rosemary grilled veal steaks

preparation time 10 minutes
cooking time 15 minutes
serves 4

2 tablespoons olive oil
2 tablespoons balsamic vinegar
1 tablespoon fresh rosemary leaves
2 cloves garlic, crushed
4 x 125g veal steaks
4 medium egg tomatoes (300g), halved
4 flat mushrooms (320g)

1 Combine oil, vinegar, rosemary, garlic and veal in medium bowl.
2 Cook veal on heated oiled grill plate (or grill or barbecue), brushing occasionally with vinegar mixture, until cooked as desired. Remove from heat; cover to keep warm.
3 Cook tomato and mushrooms on heated oiled grill plate until tender. Serve veal with grilled vegetables.

per serving 11.3g total fat (1.8g saturated fat); 1016kJ (243 cal); 2.1g carbohydrate; 31.6g protein; 3.3g fibre

Pork fillet and pancetta kebabs

preparation time 15 minutes
cooking time 15 minutes
serves 4

barbecue & grill

8 x 15cm stalks fresh rosemary
600g pork fillet, cut into 2cm pieces
8 slices pancetta (120g), halved
1 large red capsicum (350g), cut into 24 pieces
⅓ cup (80ml) olive oil
1 clove garlic, crushed

1 Remove leaves from bottom two thirds of each
rosemary stalk; reserve 2 tablespoons leaves, chop
finely. Sharpen trimmed ends of stalks to a point.
2 Wrap each piece of pork in one slice of
the pancetta; thread with capsicum, alternately,
onto stalks.
3 Brush kebabs with combined chopped rosemary,
oil and garlic. Cook on heated oiled grill plate (or
grill or barbecue), brushing frequently with
rosemary mixture, until cooked.

per serving 23.6g total fat (4.4g saturated fat);
1601kJ (383 cal); 3.1g carbohydrate;
39.5g protein; 1g fibre

goes well with greek salad.

13

Herbed rib-eye with tapenade mash

preparation time 10 minutes
cooking time 25 minutes
serves 4

4 large potatoes (1.2kg), chopped coarsely
1 tablespoon dried italian herbs
1 clove garlic, crushed
2 tablespoons olive oil
4 x 200g beef rib-eye steaks
½ cup (125ml) cream
2 tablespoons black olive tapenade
60g baby rocket leaves

1 Boil, steam or microwave potato until tender; drain. Cover to keep warm.
2 Meanwhile, combine herbs, garlic, oil and beef in medium bowl.
3 Cook beef on heated oiled grill plate (or grill or barbecue), brushing occasionally with herb mixture, until cooked as desired. Remove from heat, cover; stand 5 minutes.
4 Mash potato in large bowl with cream and tapenade. Stir in half the rocket.
5 Serve beef with mash and remaining rocket.

per serving 34g total fat (14.3g saturated fat); 2930kJ (761 cal); 41.1g carbohydrate; 54.6g protein; 6.4g fibre

500g uncooked medium king prawns
250g scallops, roe removed
2 teaspoons olive oil
3 cloves garlic, crushed
340g asparagus, halved crossways
150g sugar snap peas, trimmed
2 teaspoons lemon juice
2 tablespoons dry white wine
¾ cup (180ml) cream
2 tablespoons coarsely chopped fresh parsley

1 Shell and devein prawns, leaving tails intact; combine with scallops, oil and garlic in medium bowl.
2 Cook seafood on heated oiled grill plate (or grill or barbecue) until changed in colour. Remove from heat; cover to keep warm.
3 Meanwhile, boil, steam or microwave asparagus and peas, separately, until tender. Drain; cover to keep warm.
4 Simmer juice and wine in small saucepan, uncovered, about 1 minute or until reduced by half. Add cream; bring to a boil. Reduce heat; simmer, uncovered, 2 minutes. Add seafood; simmer, uncovered, until hot.
5 Serve seafood with vegetables, sprinkled with chopped parsley.

per serving 22.7g total fat (13.4g saturated fat); 1367kJ (327 cal); 4.6g carbohydrate; 23.7g protein; 2.2g fibre

Seafood in lemon cream sauce

preparation time 15 minutes
cooking time 10 minutes
serves 4

16

Char-grilled radicchio parcels

preparation time 20 minutes
cooking time 5 minutes
serves 4

3 cloves garlic, crushed
1 cup (150g) drained semi-dried tomatoes,
    chopped coarsely
420g bocconcini cheese
1 cup coarsely chopped fresh basil
2 x 420g cans white beans, rinsed, drained
24 large radicchio leaves
1 tablespoon balsamic vinegar

1 Combine garlic, tomato, cheese, basil and beans
in large bowl.
2 Plunge radicchio into large saucepan of boiling
water then drain immediately; submerge in iced
water to halt cooking process. When cool, drain; pat
dry with absorbent paper.
3 Slightly overlap 2 leaves; centre about a quarter
cup of bean mixture on leaves then roll, folding in
edges to enclose filling. Repeat with remaining bean
mixture and leaves.
4 Cook parcels, seam-side down, on heated oiled
grill plate (or grill or barbecue) until filling is hot.
Serve parcels drizzled with vinegar.
per serving 20g total fat (11g saturated fat);
1659kJ (397 cal); 18.9g carbohydrate;
28.7g protein; 13.8g fibre

Teriyaki salmon with soba salad

preparation time 10 minutes
cooking time 15 minutes
serves 4

250g dried soba noodles
4 x 200g salmon fillets
¼ cup (60ml) teriyaki sauce
2 tablespoons sweet chilli sauce
1 medium red capsicum (200g), sliced thinly
4 green onions, sliced thinly
1 tablespoon light soy sauce
2 teaspoons lime juice
1 teaspoon sesame oil

1 Cook noodles in large saucepan of boiling water, uncovered, until just tender; drain. Rinse under cold water; drain.
2 Meanwhile, combine salmon, teriyaki sauce, and 1 tablespoon of the sweet chilli sauce in medium bowl.
3 Cook salmon on heated oiled grill plate (or grill or barbecue), brushing occasionally with teriyaki mixture, until cooked as desired.
4 Combine noodles with remaining ingredients in large bowl. Serve soba with salmon, and lime wedges, if you like.

per serving 16.4g total fat (3.5g saturated fat); 2249kJ (538 cal); 47.4g carbohydrate; 48g protein; 3.2g fibre

Pesto chicken with grilled zucchini

preparation time 10 minutes
cooking time 15 minutes
serves 4

6 medium zucchini (720g),
  sliced thickly lengthways
2 tablespoons olive oil
1 clove garlic, crushed
1 tablespoon finely chopped fresh basil
1 teaspoon finely grated lemon rind
⅓ cup (90g) sun-dried tomato pesto
2 tablespoons chicken stock
4 x 200g chicken thigh fillets, cut into thirds

1 Cook zucchini on heated oiled grill plate (or grill or barbecue), in batches, until tender. Combine with oil, garlic, basil and rind in medium bowl; cover to keep warm.
2 Combine pesto, stock and chicken in large bowl. Cook chicken on heated oiled grill plate (or grill or barbecue), brushing occasionally with pesto mixture, until cooked. Serve chicken with zucchini.
per serving 33.1g total fat (7.6g saturated fat); 2611kJ (481 cal); 3.3g carbohydrate; 41.7g protein; 3.6g fibre

goes well with baby rocket leaves.

19

Wok

baby buk choy

No longer just the province of the Chinese greengrocer, leafy Asian vegetables like baby buk choy and gai lan are found in most supermarkets, on restaurant menus and in our refrigerator crispers at home. Baby buk choy is particularly popular, and no wonder – it's fairly inexpensive, easy to prepare, full of nutrients and absolutely delicious. Plus, wok-tossed with either a little sesame oil or oyster sauce, it can be on the table in a dash.

fresh rice noodles

Fresh rice noodles can be found under various names – ho fun, sen yau, pho or kway tiau, depending on the nationality of the manufacturer. Used throughout South-East Asia, this noodle can be purchased in various widths or large sheets weighing about 500g that are cut into the desired size. Chewy and pure white, they don't have to be pre-cooked in boiling water before being tossed in a wok with a recipe's various other ingredients.

hoisin sauce

Hoisin sauce is a thick, sweet Chinese barbecue sauce made from salted fermented soybeans, onion, sugar, white vinegar, garlic and chillies. It can be used as a marinade or a baste (traditional for suckling pig), or as a flavouring or dipping sauce for stir-fried, braised or roasted foods. It is always traditionally served with Peking duck. Found in all Asian food shops and most supermarkets, a dollop of hoisin sauce adds oomph to any stir-fry.

red thai chilli

There are a great many varieties of chilli used in Thai cooking – different ones are used for different dishes – but the most well known must be "prik kee noo", a very short, small red capsicum variety we call the red thai chilli, or "scud", which helps identify its heat quotient. Averaging 3cm in length, it is one of the hottest members of the chilli family. Seed the chillies to lessen their intensity but wear disposable kitchen gloves when doing so.

Lamb teriyaki with broccolini

preparation time 10 minutes
cooking time 15 minutes
serves 4

1 tablespoon vegetable oil
800g lamb strips
4 green onions, chopped coarsely
3cm piece fresh ginger (15g), grated
175g broccolini, chopped coarsely
150g green beans, trimmed, halved crossways
⅓ cup (80ml) teriyaki sauce
2 tablespoons honey
2 teaspoons sesame oil
1 tablespoon roasted sesame seeds

1 Heat half the vegetable oil in wok; stir-fry lamb, in batches, until browned.
2 Heat remaining vegetable oil in wok; stir-fry onion and ginger until onion softens. Add broccolini and beans; stir-fry until vegetables are tender. Remove from wok.
3 Add sauce, honey and sesame oil to wok; bring to a boil. Boil, uncovered, about 3 minutes or until sauce thickens slightly. Return lamb and vegetables to wok; stir-fry until hot. Sprinkle with seeds.

per serving 15.9g total fat (4.3g saturated fat); 1626kJ (389 cal); 14.1g carbohydrate; 45.7g protein; 3.4g fibre

goes well with steamed rice.

Green curry chicken with baby eggplant

preparation time 10 minutes
cooking time 20 minutes
serves 4

2 tablespoons vegetable oil
6 baby eggplants (360g), sliced thickly
1 large red onion (300g), sliced thinly
150g mushrooms, halved
2 tablespoons green curry paste
1 teaspoon cumin seeds
1 fresh small red thai chilli, sliced thinly
1 cup (250ml) coconut milk
600g chicken tenderloins, chopped coarsely
½ cup loosely packed fresh coriander leaves

1 Heat half the oil in wok; stir-fry eggplant, onion and mushrooms, in batches, until vegetables are tender.
2 Heat remaining oil in wok; stir-fry paste, seeds and chilli until fragrant. Add coconut milk and chicken; stir-fry until chicken is cooked through. Return vegetables to wok; stir-fry until hot. Sprinkle with coriander.

per serving 34.4g total fat (15.4g saturated fat); 2128kJ (509 cal); 9.9g carbohydrate; 37.5g protein; 6.4g fibre

goes well with naan bread.

Ginger-plum chicken and noodle stir-fry

preparation time 10 minutes
cooking time 15 minutes
serves 4

We used a 400g packet of prepared asian stir-fry vegetables for this recipe, available from supermarkets.

2 tablespoons vegetable oil
600g chicken breast fillets, sliced thinly
450g hokkien noodles
1 medium brown onion (150g), sliced thinly
1 clove garlic, crushed
3cm piece fresh ginger (15g), grated
400g packaged fresh asian stir-fry vegetables
2 tablespoons sweet chilli sauce
2 tablespoons plum sauce

1 Heat half the oil in wok; stir-fry chicken, in batches, until browned.
2 Meanwhile, place noodles in medium heatproof bowl, cover with boiling water; separate with fork, drain.
3 Heat remaining oil in wok; stir-fry onion, garlic and ginger until onion softens. Add vegetables; stir-fry until just tender. Return chicken to wok with noodles and sauces; stir-fry until hot.
per serving 19.4g total fat (4.6g saturated fat); 2784kJ (666 cal); 73.3g carbohydrate; 45.6g protein; 6.2g fibre

Chilli, salt and pepper seafood

preparation time 15 minutes
cooking time 15 minutes
serves 4

500g uncooked medium king prawns
300g cleaned squid hoods
300g scallops, roe removed
2 teaspoons sea salt
½ teaspoon cracked black pepper
½ teaspoon five-spice powder
2 fresh small red thai chillies, chopped finely
2 tablespoons peanut oil
150g sugar snap peas, trimmed
2 tablespoons light soy sauce
1 lime, cut into wedges

1 Shell and devein prawns, leaving tails intact. Cut squid down centre to open out; score inside in diagonal pattern then cut into thick strips.
2 Combine seafood, salt, pepper, five-spice and chilli in large bowl.
3 Heat half the oil in wok; stir-fry seafood, in batches, until cooked.
4 Heat remaining oil in wok; stir-fry peas until tender. Return seafood to wok with sauce; stir-fry until hot. Serve seafood with lime.

per serving 11g total fat (2.2g saturated fat); 1070kJ (256 cal); 2.7g carbohydrate; 35.8g protein; 1.2g fibre

Javanese stir-fried pork and rice noodles

preparation time 10 minutes
cooking time 15 minutes
serves 4

450g fresh wide rice noodles
1 tablespoon vegetable oil
500g pork mince
2 cloves garlic, crushed
1 tablespoon sambal oelek
4 green onions, sliced thinly
⅓ cup (80ml) kecap manis
2 baby buk choy (300g), leaves separated
1 cup loosely packed fresh coriander leaves

1 Place noodles in large heatproof bowl, cover with boiling water; separate with fork, drain.
2 Heat oil in wok; stir-fry pork until browned. Add garlic, sambal, onion and 1 tablespoon of the kecap manis; stir-fry 1 minute.
3 Add noodles, remaining kecap manis and buk choy to wok; stir-fry until hot. Sprinkle with coriander.

per serving 14.5g total fat (3.8g saturated fat); 1927kJ (461 cal); 49g carbohydrate; 31.1g protein; 2.8g fibre

Tofu, cashew and vegie stir-fry

preparation time 5 minutes
cooking time 10 minutes
serves 4

We used cryovac-packed ready-to-serve sweet chilli tofu, available from many supermarkets and Asian food stores.
Packaged fresh stir-fry vegies are available from supermarkets.

1 tablespoon vegetable oil
1 fresh long red chilli, sliced thinly
500g packaged fresh stir-fry vegetables
400g packaged marinated tofu pieces, chopped coarsely
½ cup (75g) roasted unsalted cashews
⅓ cup (80ml) hoisin sauce
1 tablespoon lime juice

1 Heat oil in wok; stir-fry chilli, vegetables, tofu and nuts until vegetables are just tender.
2 Add sauce and juice; stir-fry until hot.
per serving 22.6g total fat (3.4g saturated fat); 1563kJ (374 cal); 20.9g carbohydrate; 18.2g protein; 8.4g fibre

goes well with steamed rice.

Mussels in black bean sauce

preparation time 10 minutes
cooking time 10 minutes
serves 4

2kg medium black mussels
1 tablespoon peanut oil
6cm piece fresh ginger (30g), sliced thinly
4 cloves garlic, sliced thinly
8 green onions, sliced thinly
4 fresh small red thai chillies, chopped finely
⅓ cup (100g) black bean sauce
¼ cup (60ml) fish stock
¼ cup (60ml) water
1 cup firmly packed fresh coriander leaves

1 Scrub mussels under cold water; remove beards.
2 Heat oil in wok; stir-fry ginger, garlic, onion and chilli until fragrant. Add sauce, stock and the water; bring to a boil.
3 Add mussels; simmer, covered, about 5 minutes or until mussels open (discard any that do not). Remove from heat; sprinkle with coriander.

per serving 8.4g total fat (1g saturated fat); 882kJ (211 cal); 9.4g carbohydrate; 23.2g protein; 2.1g fibre

goes well with steamed rice.

Char siu pork, corn and choy sum

preparation time 10 minutes
cooking time 15 minutes
serves 4

2 tablespoons peanut oil
600g pork fillets, sliced thinly
2 medium brown onions (300g), cut into
   thin wedges
230g baby corn
300g choy sum, trimmed, chopped coarsely
2 tablespoons char siu sauce
2 teaspoons light soy sauce
2 teaspoons lime juice
1 fresh long red chilli, sliced thinly

1 Heat half the oil in wok; stir-fry pork, in batches,
until browned.
2 Heat remaining oil in wok; stir-fry onion and
corn until onion softens.
3 Return pork to wok with choy sum, sauces and
juice; stir-fry until hot. Sprinkle with chilli.

per serving 14g total fat (3g saturated fat);
1513kJ (362cal); 18.4g carbohydrate;
37.5g protein; 5.7g fibre

Beef kway teo

preparation time 10 minutes
cooking time 10 minutes
serves 4

Garlic chives have rougher, flatter leaves than simple
chives, and possess a pink-tinged teardrop-shaped
flowering bud at the end. They can be used as a
salad green, or steamed and eaten as a vegetable.

¼ cup (60ml) oyster sauce
2 tablespoons kecap manis
2 tablespoons chinese cooking wine
1 teaspoon sambal oelek
3 cloves garlic, crushed
2cm piece fresh ginger (10g), grated
2 tablespoons peanut oil
500g beef strips
450g fresh wide rice noodles
6 green onions, cut into 2cm lengths
1 medium red capsicum (200g), sliced thinly
¼ cup (15g) coarsely chopped garlic chives
2 cups (160g) bean sprouts

1 Combine sauce, kecap manis, cooking wine,
sambal, garlic and ginger in small jug.
2 Heat half the oil in wok; stir-fry beef, in batches,
until browned.
3 Meanwhile, place noodles in large heatproof bowl,
cover with boiling water; separate with fork, drain.
4 Heat remaining oil in wok; stir-fry onion and
capsicum until capsicum is tender.
5 Return beef to wok with sauce mixture, noodles,
chives and sprouts; stir-fry until hot.
per serving 21.8g total fat (6.8g saturated fat);
2362kJ (565 cal); 54.2g carbohydrate;
33.7g protein; 3.6g fibre

Chilli fried rice with chicken and broccolini

preparation time 10 minutes
cooking time 15 minutes
serves 4

You need to cook 1 cup (200g) white long-grain rice for this recipe.
You need a large barbecued chicken, weighing approximately 900g, for this recipe.

1 tablespoon peanut oil
3 eggs, beaten lightly
1 medium brown onion (150g), sliced thinly
1 clove garlic, crushed
2 fresh long red chillies, sliced thinly
175g broccolini, chopped coarsely
2 cups (320g) shredded barbecued chicken
3 cups cooked white long-grain rice
1 tablespoon light soy sauce
1 tablespoon hoisin sauce

1 Heat about a third of the oil in wok; add half the egg, swirl wok to make a thin omelette. Remove omelette from wok; roll then cut into thin strips. Repeat process using another third of the oil and remaining egg.
2 Heat remaining oil in wok; stir-fry onion, garlic and chilli until onion softens. Add broccolini; stir-fry until tender.
3 Add remaining ingredients to wok; stir-fry until hot. Add omelette; toss gently.
per serving 15.3g total fat (3.8g saturated fat); 1881kJ (450 cal); 44.6g carbohydrate; 30.9g protein; 4.1g fibre

Portuguese prawn and chorizo sauté

preparation time 15 minutes
cooking time 10 minutes
serves 4

500g uncooked medium king prawns,
   shelled, deveined
2 chorizo sausages (340g), sliced thinly
1 large red onion (300g), chopped coarsely
2 medium red capsicums (400g), chopped coarsely
1 teaspoon sweet smoked paprika
2 tablespoons red wine vinegar
1 teaspoon finely grated orange rind
2 teaspoons olive oil
1 medium orange (240g), segmented
1 cup loosely packed fresh flat-leaf parsley leaves

1 Combine prawns, chorizo, onion, capsicum,
paprika, vinegar and rind in large bowl.
2 Heat oil in wok; stir-fry prawn mixture until
vegetables are tender.
3 Remove from heat; add orange and parsley,
toss to combine.

per serving 28.5g total fat (9.6g saturated fat);
1852kJ (443 cal); 13g carbohydrate;
32.5g protein; 3.9g fibre

goes well with green salad and crusty bread.

Pot & Pan

ready-made ravioli

A boon for the working cook, refrigerated or frozen ravioli, available in supermarkets and delicatessens, are machine-made or handmade small filled pasta cases made from durum wheat semolina and fresh eggs then stuffed with meat, cheese or vegetables. These are cooked in large pots of boiling water and served with various sauces and cheese, just like dried unfilled pasta. Two other shapes are sold alongside ravioli, and all are interchangeable with one another: agnolotti ("lamb ears" in Italian) are a small round piece of flattened pasta dough, folded over a meat and vegetable stuffing into a half-moon shape; and tortellini, round pasta cases similarly filled then twisted into ring shapes.

tomato pasta sauce

Another wonderful pantry staple: some of the better bottled pasta sauces around today are virtually indistinguishable from homemade. Use the simplest ones, those made only from cooked-down fresh tomatoes with, perhaps, a bit of chilli, basil or onion added. As a base for your next bolognese or napoletana dish or pizza topping, it's best to start with a plain sauce and spunk it up yourself. Many good varieties are imported and are sold under their Italian names such as sugo, ragù or passata. Cheaper sauces are usually made with dried herbs or flavour enhancers that can alter the taste of your finished dish. Unused sauce will keep for a week or so, stored tightly sealed in a glass jar in your fridge.

pancetta

An Italian style of bacon, pancetta is lean salted pork belly that is cured but not smoked, flavoured with salt, pepper and other spices, then rolled into a fat sausage-like loaf. It is usually only used to impart flavour to pasta sauces and meat dishes. There are many varieties, with each region of Italy producing its own version of pancetta. Its place of origin is believed to be Corsica, and there it is frequently eaten on its own, like prosciutto or ham, on an antipasto platter. Pasta (traditionally bucatini) all'amatriciana, a robust pancetta and tomato sauce, is the one most people think of when cooking with pancetta, but it adds its spicy salty signature to traditional Italian egg and vegetable dishes, too.

baby spinach leaves

These tender, fresh leaves, sold loose or packed in cellophane, have become a salad favourite, rivalling rocket for top spot on the baby greens list. Tossed with a simple lemon and oil dressing with tomatoes, nuts, bacon or parmesan, they make a divine side salad. Uncooked baby spinach is also perfect sprinkled over a just-baked pizza or stirred into a finished soup, risotto, stir-fry or pasta sauce just before serving, the trick being to allow the leaves to barely wilt. Baby spinach leaves are more tender than the large spinach sometimes erroneously called English spinach, which is sold in bunches. This low-kilojoule vegetable is not just high in folate, vitamin C, anti-oxidants and fibre – it's also delicious.

Pancetta and radicchio rigatoni

preparation time 10 minutes
cooking time 15 minutes
serves 4

Rigatoni, a stocky, tubular pasta with a ridged exterior, is ideal for this recipe because the filling clings both to the grooves on the pasta as well as within the hollow. Penne pasta is an acceptable substitute, if you like.

500g rigatoni pasta
6 slices pancetta (90g)
20g butter
1 medium leek (350g), sliced thinly
1 cup (250ml) cream
2 medium radicchio (400g), trimmed, sliced thinly
½ cup loosely packed fresh flat-leaf parsley leaves
2 teaspoons finely grated lemon rind
⅓ cup (80ml) lemon juice

1 Cook pasta in large saucepan of boiling water, uncovered, until tender.
2 Meanwhile, cook pancetta in heated oiled large frying pan until crisp. Drain on absorbent paper; chop coarsely.
3 Melt butter in same frying pan; cook leek, stirring, until soft. Add cream; bring to a boil. Reduce heat; simmer, uncovered, 2 minutes.
4 Add leek mixture to drained pasta with half the pancetta and remaining ingredients; toss gently then sprinkle with remaining pancetta.

per serving 34.4g total fat (21.3g saturated fat); 3252kJ (778 cal); 96.9g carbohydrate; 22g protein; 8.2g fibre

Pork, kumara mash and apple salsa

preparation time 10 minutes
cooking time 20 minutes
serves 4

2 large kumara (1kg), chopped coarsely
20g butter
2 tablespoons finely chopped fresh sage
4 x 200g pork butterfly steaks
1 tablespoon olive oil
2 cloves garlic, crushed

apple salsa

1 large green apple (200g), chopped finely
1 small red onion (100g), chopped finely
1 clove garlic, crushed
1 tablespoon finely chopped fresh sage
1 tablespoon olive oil

1 Make apple salsa.
2 Boil, steam or microwave kumara until tender; drain. Mash kumara with butter in large bowl until smooth; stir in half the sage.
3 Meanwhile, combine pork, oil, garlic and remaining sage in large bowl.
4 Cook pork in heated oiled grill pan until browned. Serve with mash and salsa.

apple salsa Combine ingredients in small bowl.

per serving 34.1g total fat (10.8g saturated fat); 3327kJ (796 cal); 65.8g carbohydrate; 51.5g protein; 9.1g fibre

Ravioli with tomato, pea and basil sauce

preparation time 10 minutes
cooking time 15 minutes
serves 4

2 teaspoons olive oil
6 slices pancetta (90g)
1 clove garlic, crushed
700g bottled tomato pasta sauce
¼ cup (60ml) dry white wine
2 tablespoons finely chopped fresh basil
1 cup (120g) frozen peas
625g spinach and ricotta ravioli

1 Heat oil in large frying pan; cook pancetta until crisp. Drain on absorbent paper; break into pieces.
2 Cook garlic in same pan, stirring, 1 minute. Add sauce, wine and basil; bring to a boil. Add peas, reduce heat; simmer, uncovered, 15 minutes.
3 Meanwhile, cook ravioli in large saucepan of boiling water, uncovered, until just tender; drain. Return ravioli to pan, add sauce; toss to combine. Divide among serving bowls; top with pancetta.

per serving 12.8g total fat (4.1g saturated fat); 1593kJ (381 cal); 46.6g carbohydrate; 20.1g protein; 7.4g fibre

Chicken, lentil and cauliflower pilaf

preparation time 10 minutes
cooking time 20 minutes
serves 4

Formerly known as Madras, the southeast Indian city of Chennai is the traditional home of this aromatic and spicy curry paste made from coriander, chilli, cinnamon and cumin.

1 medium brown onion (150g), sliced thinly
1 clove garlic, crushed
2 tablespoons madras curry paste
1 cup (200g) basmati rice
½ small cauliflower (500g), cut into florets
400g can brown lentils, rinsed, drained
1 cup (250ml) chicken stock
1 cup (250ml) water
2 cups (320g) coarsely chopped barbecued chicken
½ cup firmly packed fresh coriander leaves

1 Cook onion and garlic in heated oiled large frying pan until onion softens. Add paste; cook, stirring, about 5 minutes or until fragrant.
2 Add rice, cauliflower and lentils; stir to coat in onion mixture. Add stock, the water and chicken; bring to a boil. Reduce heat; simmer, covered tightly, about 15 minutes or until rice is tender and liquid has been absorbed. Remove from heat; fluff pilaf with fork. Stir in coriander; serve with lime wedges, pappadums and chutney, if you like.
per serving 10.7g total fat (2.3g saturated fat); 1814kJ (434 cal); 50.2g carbohydrate; 36.6g protein; 6.1g fibre

tip
Buy a barbecued chicken weighing approximately 900g on your way home from work; skin and bone it then chop the meat to get the right amount of chicken required for this recipe.

Lamb cutlets niçoise

preparation time 10 minutes
cooking time 20 minutes
serves 4

12 french-trimmed lamb cutlets (600g)
1 large cos lettuce, chopped coarsely
420g can white beans, rinsed, drained
3 medium tomatoes (450g), cut into wedges
lemon anchovy dressing
4 anchovy fillets, drained, chopped finely
3 cloves garlic, crushed
3 teaspoons finely grated lemon rind
⅓ cup (80ml) lemon juice
⅓ cup (80ml) olive oil

1 Make lemon anchovy dressing.
2 Combine lamb and 2 tablespoons of the dressing in large bowl.
3 Cook lamb in heated oiled large frying pan, uncovered, in batches, until cooked as desired. Remove from heat; drizzle with 1 tablespoon of the dressing, cover to keep warm.
4 Combine remaining dressing, lettuce, beans and tomato in large bowl. Serve lamb with salad.
lemon anchovy dressing Combine ingredients in screw-top jar; shake well.
per serving 33g total fat (8.8g saturated fat); 1852kJ (443 cal); 9.9g carbohydrate; 24.8g protein; 5.2g fibre

Pan-fried blue-eye with fennel salad

preparation time 10 minutes
cooking time 10 minutes
serves 4

4 x 200g blue-eye fillets, skin-on
2 medium red capsicums (400g), chopped coarsely
2 small fennel (400g), trimmed, sliced thinly
½ cup (60g) seeded black olives
⅓ cup coarsely chopped fresh basil
2 tablespoons olive oil
1 tablespoon balsamic vinegar

1 Cook fish, skin-side down, in heated oiled large frying pan, turning once, until cooked.
2 Meanwhile, combine remaining ingredients in medium bowl. Serve fish with salad.

per serving 13.9g total fat (2.7g saturated fat); 1409kJ (337 cal); 8.6g carbohydrate; 42.9g protein; 2.8g fibre

Peppered fillet steaks with creamy bourbon sauce

preparation time 5 minutes
cooking time 15 minutes
serves 4

4 x 125g beef fillet steaks
2 teaspoons cracked black pepper
2 tablespoons olive oil
6 shallots (150g), sliced thinly
1 clove garlic, crushed
⅓ cup (80ml) bourbon
¼ cup (60ml) beef stock
2 teaspoons dijon mustard
300ml cream

1 Rub beef all over with pepper. Heat half the oil in large frying pan; cook beef, uncovered, until cooked as desired. Remove from pan; cover to keep warm.
2 Heat remaining oil in same pan; cook shallot and garlic, stirring, until shallot softens. Add bourbon; stir until mixture simmers and starts to thicken. Add remaining ingredients; bring to a boil. Reduce heat; simmer, uncovered, about 5 minutes or until sauce thickens slightly.
3 Serve beef drizzled with sauce.
per serving 49.3g total fat (25.9g saturated fat); 2742kJ (656 cal); 13.2g carbohydrate; 28.7g protein; 0.7g fibre

goes well with oven-baked chips and green beans.

Chicken, tomato and fetta patties with spinach salad

preparation time 20 minutes
cooking time 10 minutes
serves 4

750g chicken mince
⅓ cup (50g) drained semi-dried tomatoes,
    chopped coarsely
1 egg
½ cup (35g) stale breadcrumbs
200g fetta cheese, crumbled
1 small white onion (80g) sliced thinly
100g baby spinach leaves
1 tablespoon olive oil
1 tablespoon balsamic vinegar

1 Combine chicken, tomato, egg, breadcrumbs
and half the cheese in large bowl; shape mixture
into 12 patties.
2 Cook patties in heated oiled large frying pan,
in batches, until cooked through. Drain on
absorbent paper.
3 Meanwhile, combine onion, spinach, oil, vinegar
and remaining cheese in medium bowl. Serve
patties with spinach salad.
per serving 33.7g total fat (13.3g saturated fat);
2320kJ (555 cal); 11.8g carbohydrate;
50.1g protein; 3.2g fibre

Spicy veal pizzaiola

preparation time 10 minutes
cooking time 20 minutes
serves 4

The pizzaiola sauce recipe makes enough to accompany 375g of the cooked pasta of your choice, or you can cover and reserve it in the fridge for use within three days.

2 tablespoons olive oil
2 cloves garlic, crushed
4 slices pancetta (60g), chopped finely
¼ cup (60ml) dry white wine
700g bottled tomato pasta sauce
1 teaspoon dried chilli flakes
4 x 170g veal cutlets
75g baby spinach leaves

1 Heat 2 teaspoons of the oil in large saucepan; cook garlic and pancetta, stirring, about 5 minutes. Add wine; cook, stirring, until wine is reduced by half. Add sauce and chilli; simmer, uncovered, about 15 minutes or until sauce thickens.
2 Meanwhile, heat remaining oil in large frying pan. Cook veal, uncovered, until cooked as desired.
3 Remove sauce from heat; stir in spinach. Top veal with sauce.

per serving 14.6g total fat (2.8g saturated fat); 1555kJ (372 cal); 18.8g carbohydrate; 36.3g protein; 4.3g fibre

goes well with pasta.

Pumpkin and sage ravioli

preparation time 10 minutes
cooking time 15 minutes
serves 4

¼ cup (40g) pine nuts
2 teaspoons olive oil
3 cloves garlic, crushed
600g piece pumpkin, cut into 1cm cubes
625g ricotta ravioli
300ml cream
¼ cup (20g) finely grated parmesan cheese
2 tablespoons coarsely chopped fresh sage
2 tablespoons lemon juice

1 Cook nuts in large frying pan, stirring, until browned lightly; remove from pan.
2 Heat oil in same pan; cook garlic and pumpkin, covered, stirring occasionally, about 10 minutes or until pumpkin is almost tender.
3 Meanwhile, cook ravioli in large saucepan of boiling water, uncovered, until just tender; drain.
4 Add nuts, cream, cheese and sage to pumpkin mixture; bring to a boil. Reduce heat; simmer, uncovered, 5 minutes. Add ravioli and juice; stir until hot.

per serving 51.7g total fat (26.7g saturated fat); 2826kJ (676 cal); 32.5g carbohydrate; 19.2g protein; 4.7g fibre

Green bean and pesto frittata

preparation time 10 minutes
cooking time 20 minutes
serves 4

1 tablespoon olive oil
1 large potato (300g), cut into 1cm cubes
1 large brown onion (200g), sliced thinly
400g green beans, trimmed, chopped coarsely
10 eggs
⅓ cup (90g) basil pesto
⅓ cup finely chopped fresh basil
½ cup (40g) finely grated parmesan cheese

1 Heat oil in 28cm frying pan; cook potato, onion and beans, covered, stirring occasionally, until vegetables soften.
2 Whisk eggs lightly in large bowl, whisk in pesto and chopped basil. Pour egg mixture over vegetables; sprinkle with cheese. Cook frittata, uncovered, over low heat until almost set.
3 Meanwhile, preheat grill. Place pan under grill (shielding handle with foil, if necessary) until cheese melts. Remove from heat; stand 10 minutes.

per serving 30.2g total fat (8.7g saturated fat); 1889kJ (452 cal); 15.6g carbohydrate; 27.4g protein; 5.5g fibre

goes well with green salad.

51

Roast & Bake

french-trimmed lamb racks

A 4-cutlet french-trimmed lamb rack is what is usually considered a one-serving portion, but this really depends on the content of your meal. You can up-size to a roasted 6-cutlet rack served with a simple salad, or revert to a grilled 2-cutlet rack if it's to follow an entrée and accompany a few sides. To "french" a rack or cutlet, rib or shank, is short for "to cut in the French manner", which is when the upper ends of the bones are cut and trimmed of all gristle, fat and even meat, to expose the cleaned bone. Frenching racks gives the diner practically nothing but pure luscious meat to eat, and it is as visually appealing as it is a healthy technique, since most of the meat's fat has been cut away.

wholegrain mustard

A coarse-grained mustard usually made from a blend of whole black and yellow mustard seeds, spices and vinegar. These days, there are many permutations of the original, some being flavoured with honey, crushed green peppercorns, citrus or red wine. It's good to keep on hand as it not only adds flavour but texture, too, to dressings and sauces. It keeps better than straight dijon, but must be stored tightly sealed to prevent air from affecting it. Rustic and hearty, smooth with a decided spice hit to it, this old-fashioned mustard adds zest to gravies and marinades, and is great when accompanying a platter of cold roast meat or chicken, baked ham, pâtés and smoked meats.

baby fennel

Slim baby fennel, also known as finocchio or anise, are slightly flat, and not as bulb-shaped as the adult version. Picked at a young age with the fronds attached, they can weigh as little as 100g and be not much larger than a carrot: as a rule of thumb, the smaller, the more tender and flavourful. Braised alongside roasting meat, particularly veal and pork, or baked au gratin with cream and cheese, their distinct licorice flavour becomes more delicate and sweeter. Baby fennel can be sliced or shaved and eaten raw in a salad or on a crudités platter; they also stand up to strong Mediterranean flavours like parmesan and pecorino cheeses, olives, roasted red capsicum, saffron, bay leaf and thyme.

baby truss tomatoes

Small, even tiny, vine-ripened tomatoes are referred to as trussed or trellised when they're sold still attached on the vine to one another. Presented as a "bunch", like a bunch of grapes, they make a stunning showpiece: their striking red skin and bright green calyx are matched in appeal by their firm, crisp texture and robust flavour. Roast and serve them, still trussed and brushed with garlic-scented olive oil, alongside a leg of lamb or a whole beef fillet. They can also be quickly softened in a hot oven and served with fresh mozzarella and baby basil leaves as a taste-tempting caprese salad. Only buy trussed tomatoes shortly before you intend using them, and leave them at room temperature.

Chorizo and white bean braise

preparation time 10 minutes
cooking time 25 minutes
serves 4

You need about 1kg of untrimmed silver beet to get the amount needed for this recipe.

4 chorizo sausages (680g), sliced thickly
2 cloves garlic, sliced thinly
2 baby fennel (260g), trimmed, chopped coarsely
400g can chopped tomatoes
⅓ cup (80ml) chicken stock
2 x 420g cans white beans, rinsed, drained
1 cup (250ml) water
250g trimmed silver beet, chopped coarsely

1 Preheat oven to 200°C/180°C fan-forced.
2 Cook chorizo in heated large flameproof dish, stirring, about 5 minutes. Add garlic and fennel; cook, stirring, 2 minutes.
3 Add undrained tomatoes, stock, beans and the water; cook, in oven, uncovered, 15 minutes. Stir in silver beet; cook, uncovered, about 5 minutes or until silver beet wilts.
per serving 52g total fat (18.6g saturated fat); 3214kJ (769 cal); 24.8g carbohydrate; 44.2g protein; 14g fibre

Lime and chilli roasted snapper

preparation time 15 minutes
cooking time 15 minutes
serves 4

4 x 500g plate-size snapper, cleaned
2cm piece fresh ginger (10g), sliced thinly
2 cloves garlic, sliced thinly
8 fresh kaffir lime leaves
1 fresh long red chilli, sliced thinly
2 tablespoons peanut oil
1 cup loosely packed fresh coriander leaves
chilli lime dressing
⅓ cup (80ml) sweet chilli sauce
¼ cup (60ml) fish sauce
¼ cup (60ml) lime juice
2 teaspoons peanut oil

1 Preheat oven to 240°C/220°C fan-forced.
2 Rinse fish inside and out under cold water; pat dry with absorbent paper.
3 Divide ginger, garlic, lime leaves and chilli among fish cavities; rub fish all over with oil.
4 Place fish in two shallow oiled baking dishes; roast, uncovered, about 15 minutes or until cooked through.
5 Meanwhile, make chilli lime dressing
6 Drizzle fish with dressing, sprinkle with coriander leaves. Serve with steamed asian greens, if you like.
chilli lime dressing Combine ingredients in screw-top jar; shake well.
per serving 15.1g total fat (3.5g saturated fat); 1354kJ (324 cal); 55g carbohydrate; 40.6g protein; 1.8g fibre

tip Rubbing the kaffir lime leaves between your fingers brings out their delicate flavour.

Chicken margherita

preparation time 10 minutes
cooking time 20 minutes
serves 4

550g baby vine-ripened truss tomatoes
4 x 200g chicken breast fillets
⅓ cup (90g) basil pesto
180g bocconcini cheese, sliced thinly
20g baby spinach leaves
8 slices prosciutto (120g)

1 Preheat oven to 220°C/200°C fan-forced.
2 Remove four tomatoes from truss; slice thinly.
3 Split one chicken fillet in half horizontally; open out. Spread one tablespoon of pesto on one side of chicken fillet; top with a quarter of the cheese, a quarter of the sliced tomato and a quarter of the spinach. Fold chicken fillet over filling; wrap with two slices prosciutto to enclose securely. Repeat process with remaining chicken, pesto, cheese, sliced tomato, spinach and prosciutto.
4 Roast chicken and remaining tomatoes in large oiled shallow baking dish, uncovered, about 20 minutes or until cooked through. Serve chicken with roasted tomatoes.

per serving 28.7g total fat (10.5g saturated fat); 2144kJ (513 cal); 3g carbohydrate; 59.7g protein; 2.3g fibre

Herbed-crumbed lamb racks

preparation time 10 minutes
cooking time 20 minutes
serves 4

1 cup (70g) stale breadcrumbs
1 tablespoon finely chopped fresh flat-leaf parsley
2 tablespoons finely chopped fresh mint
2 teaspoons finely grated lemon rind
40g butter
2 shallots (50g), chopped finely
4 x 4 french-trimmed lamb cutlet racks (720g)
250g baby vine-ripened truss tomatoes
cooking-oil spray

1 Preheat oven to 220°C/200°C fan-forced.
2 Combine breadcrumbs, herbs and rind in small bowl.
3 Melt butter in small frying pan; pour half the butter into breadcrumb mixture.
4 Cook shallot in remaining butter, stirring, until soft; stir into breadcrumb mixture.
5 Place lamb and tomatoes in large lightly oiled, baking dish; spray tomatoes with oil. Press breadcrumb mixture onto lamb. Roast, uncovered, about 15 minutes or until cooked as desired. Serve lamb with roasted tomatoes.

per serving 25g total fat (12.6g saturated fat); 1538kJ (368 cal); 13.7g carbohydrate; 21.4g protein; 1.9g fibre

Lamb racks with mustard maple glaze

preparation time 10 minutes
cooking time 20 minutes
serves 4

4 x 4 french-trimmed lamb cutlet racks (720g)
2 cloves garlic, sliced thinly
2 medium parsnips (500g), cut into 2cm cubes
2 small kumara (500g), cut into 2cm cubes
½ cup loosely packed fresh flat-leaf parsley leaves
mustard maple glaze
50g butter
⅓ cup (80ml) maple syrup
2 tablespoons wholegrain mustard

1 Preheat oven to 200°C/180°C fan-forced.
2 Make mustard maple glaze.
3 Meanwhile, using sharp knife, make cuts in lamb; press garlic slices into cuts. Place lamb in large oiled baking dish; brush with 2 tablespoons of the glaze.
4 Combine remaining glaze, parsnip and kumara in medium bowl.
5 Place vegetables in baking dish with lamb; roast, uncovered, about 15 minutes or until vegetables are tender and lamb is cooked as desired. Stir parsley into vegetables; serve with lamb.

mustard maple glaze Combine ingredients in small saucepan; cook, stirring, until slightly thickened.

per serving 26.2g total fat (13.8g saturated fat); 2153kJ (515 cal); 44.4g carbohydrate; 22.8g protein; 5.5g fibre

Moroccan roasted lamb racks

preparation time 5 minutes
cooking time 20 minutes
serves 4

4 x 4 french-trimmed lamb cutlet racks (720g)
2 teaspoons ground allspice
½ teaspoon cayenne pepper
1 tablespoon olive oil
250g baby vine-ripened truss tomatoes
cooking-oil spray
1 cup firmly packed fresh mint leaves
1 small red onion (100g), sliced thinly
1 tablespoon lemon juice
⅔ cup (160g) baba ghanoush

1 Preheat oven to 220°C/200°C fan-forced.
2 Combine lamb, spices and oil in large bowl; place lamb in large shallow baking dish. Roast, uncovered, about 20 minutes or until cooked as desired. Cover; stand 5 minutes.
3 After lamb has been in oven 10 minutes, add tomatoes to dish; spray with oil. Roast about 10 minutes or until tomatoes soften.
4 Combine tomato with mint, onion and juice in medium bowl. Serve lamb with tomato salad and baba ghanoush.
per serving 29.1g total fat (9.4g saturated fat); 1605kJ (384 cal); 5.3g carbohydrate; 23g protein; 8g fibre

Baked ricotta with roast vegetables

preparation time 10 minutes
cooking time 20 minutes
serves 4

500g ricotta cheese
½ cup (40g) finely grated parmesan cheese
2 eggs
¼ cup finely chopped fresh oregano
2 teaspoons finely grated lemon rind
1 fresh small red thai chilli, chopped finely
4 baby eggplants (240g), quartered
400g baby carrots, trimmed
1 large red capsicum (350g), sliced thickly
2 tablespoons lemon juice
1 tablespoon olive oil
2 teaspoons fresh oregano leaves

1 Preheat oven to 220°C/200°C fan-forced. Oil four holes of 6-hole (¾-cup/180ml) texas muffin pan.
2 Combine cheeses, eggs, oregano, rind and chilli in medium bowl; divide mixture among pan holes. Bake, uncovered, about 20 minutes or until browned lightly and firm.
3 Meanwhile, combine eggplant, carrots, capsicum, juice and oil in large oiled shallow baking dish; roast, uncovered, 20 minutes or until tender. Sprinkle ricotta with oregano leaves; serve with vegetables.
per serving 21.7g total fat (10.5g saturated fat); 1438kJ (344 cal); 12.3g carbohydrate; 22.7g protein; 5.2g fibre

Tomato mustard beef with baby fennel

preparation time 10 minutes
cooking time 25 minutes
serves 4

½ cup (125ml) chicken stock

1 clove garlic, crushed

1kg piece beef eye-fillet, halved horizontally

4 baby fennel (520g), trimmed, halved

⅓ cup (95g) wholegrain mustard

½ cup (75g) semi-dried tomatoes, drained,
    chopped finely

1 cup (70g) stale breadcrumbs

25g butter, melted

10g butter, softened

1 teaspoon plain flour

1 tablespoon balsamic vinegar

⅓ cup (80ml) water

1 Preheat oven to 240°C/220°C fan-forced.

2 Place stock and garlic in large baking dish;
add beef and fennel.

3 Combine mustard, tomatoes, breadcrumbs and
melted butter in small bowl; press over beef. Cook
beef, uncovered, about 20 minutes or until cooked
as desired. Remove beef and fennel from pan;
cover to keep warm.

4 Blend softened butter and flour in small bowl.
Add to pan juices with vinegar and the water; bring
to a boil. Stir until sauce thickens slightly.

5 Serve beef, drizzled with sauce, with fennel.

per serving 24.7g total fat (11.3g saturated fat);
2378kJ (569 cal); 23.2g carbohydrate;
59.9g protein; 6.7g fibre

Tandoori chicken with coconut rice

preparation time 5 minutes
cooking time 25 minutes
serves 4

¼ cup (75g) tandoori paste
¼ cup (70g) yogurt
8 chicken drumsticks (1.2kg)
1¾ cups (350g) white long-grain rice
1¼ cups (310ml) hot water
400ml can coconut cream
⅓ cup loosely packed fresh coriander leaves

1 Preheat oven to 220°C/200°C fan-forced.
2 Combine paste and yogurt in large bowl. Add chicken; turn to coat in marinade.
3 Place chicken on oiled wire rack over large baking dish. Cook, uncovered, about 25 minutes or until cooked through.
4 Meanwhile, combine rice, the water and coconut cream in large saucepan; cover tightly, bring to a boil, stirring occasionally. Reduce heat; simmer, covered, about 20 minutes or until rice is tender. Remove from heat; stand, covered, 5 minutes.
5 Serve chicken and coconut rice sprinkled with coriander and, if you like, lemon wedges.

per serving 46g total fat (24.6g saturated fat); 3775kJ (903 cal); 75.2g carbohydrate; 45g protein; 4.4g fibre

Meatloaves with thai flavours

preparation time 10 minutes
cooking time 20 minutes
serves 4

600g pork mince
⅓ cup (80ml) oyster sauce
2 cloves garlic, crushed
1 egg
1 fresh small red thai chilli, chopped finely
½ cup (50g) packaged breadcrumbs
½ cup (125ml) coconut milk
⅓ cup finely chopped thai basil
250g gai lan, cut into 10cm lengths

1 Preheat oven to 240°C/220°C fan-forced.
2 Combine mince, 2 tablespoons of sauce, garlic, egg, chilli, breadcrumbs, coconut milk and basil in large bowl; shape into four rectangular meatloaves. Wrap each meatloaf in oiled foil; place in large shallow baking dish. Cook meatloaves 10 minutes.
3 Remove foil; brush meatloaves with another tablespoon of sauce. Cook, turning occasionally, about 10 minutes or until cooked through.
4 Meanwhile, boil, steam or microwave gai lan until tender; combine with remaining sauce in large bowl. Serve gai lan topped with sliced meatloaves.

per serving 16.4g total fat (7.9g saturated fat); 1496kJ (358 cal); 16.1g carbohydrate; 35.4g protein; 1.7g fibre

Veal and asparagus with basil mayo

preparation time 10 minutes
cooking time 20 minutes
serves 4

4 x 170g veal cutlets
16 fresh basil leaves
4 slices prosciutto (60g)
350g asparagus, trimmed
1 tablespoon olive oil
basil mayonnaise
½ cup (150g) mayonnaise
⅓ cup lightly packed fresh basil leaves
1 tablespoon lemon juice

1 Preheat oven to 200°C/180°C fan-forced.
2 Oil two oven trays. Place cutlets on one tray; top with basil and prosciutto (securing with toothpick if necessary). Roast, uncovered, 20 minutes or until cutlets are cooked as desired.
3 Place asparagus on remaining tray, drizzle with oil; roast, uncovered, for last 10 minutes of cutlet cooking time.
4 Meanwhile, make basil mayonnaise.
5 Serve cutlets with asparagus and mayonnaise.
basil mayonnaise Blend or process ingredients until smooth.
per serving 20.8g total fat (3.3g saturated fat); 1522kJ (364 cal); 8.5g carbohydrate; 35.3g protein; 1.2g fibre

Salad

smoked chicken

One of the most versatile and delicious ingredients to keep on hand in your refrigerator, smoked chicken provides the backbone for myriad quick after-work meals. Because, like ham, they're effectively cooked then cryovac-packed, smoked chickens have a long shelf-life and are ready-to-eat, cold or heated. Available as small whole birds or breast portions, from supermarkets and delis, smoked chicken meat marries well with many fruits and vegetables, particularly grapes, apples, celery, potatoes, mangoes, melons and avocados, and it adds a whole new dimension to macaroni or rice salad. It's also great chopped or shredded for use in pasta sauces, ravioli fillings or pizza toppings.

radicchio

Italian in origin and a member of the chicory family, radicchio's dark leaves possess a strong flavour that suits both warm or raw salads. Two varieties are eaten most often: one round like an iceberg lettuce called verona, the other, elongated like witlof, called treviso. This vegetable has gained in popularity during the past decade or so, thanks to its appearance in Italian restaurants and farmers' markets. Grilled or pan-fried then tossed with flaked parmesan, olive oil and lemon juice, radicchio stars as a first-course salad; mixed with other salad leaves and vegetables, its distinctive colour and deep, slightly bittersweet flavour turn an everyday green salad into something special.

chickpeas

Chickpeas are a major source of protein in cultures that are either predominately vegetarian or where meat is considered a luxury item. Used in many of our favourite foods (think hummus, dhal and salsa), they can be soaked, parboiled then frozen in user-friendly amounts, ready-to-go when the menu dictates. Also known as garbanzos, channa or hummus, they are available already cooked in cans; drain away the can liquid and rinse the chickpeas before using them. Full of protein and fibre, cholesterol-free and low in fat, chickpeas make a tasty and healthy addition to a salad, and go especially well with yogurt, beetroot, garlic, anchovies, lemon, mint, parsley and capers.

sweet basil

There are more than two dozen varieties of basil, but the one we usually use in our kitchens is the sweet, common, italian or genovese variety. Actually an aromatic member of the mint family, basil is always associated with the food of Italy but it's believed to have originated in India. One of the most used of the domestic herbs, basil has a great affinity with tomato and garlic: think of a salad caprese, napoletana sauce or classic bruschetta. Basil is the traditional herb used in pesto so when in season, make enough of this sauce to see you through winter; diluted with oil or lemon juice, pesto makes a marvellous salad dressing. Baby basil leaves add a zesty hint of licorice to a mixed green leaf salad.

Vietnamese duck salad

preparation time 30 minutes
serves 4

You need one whole chinese
barbecued duck for this recipe.

1kg chinese barbecued duck
1 small wombok (700g), shredded finely
1 large carrot (180g), grated coarsely
150g snow peas, sliced thinly lengthways
1 cup (80g) bean sprouts
¼ cup vietnamese mint leaves
lime dressing
½ cup (125ml) lime juice
2 tablespoons fish sauce
2 tablespoons grated palm sugar
2 fresh small red thai chillies, chopped finely

1 Make lime dressing.
2 Remove and discard skin and bones from
duck; chop meat coarsely.
3 Combine dressing, duck and remaining
ingredients in large bowl.
lime dressing Combine ingredients in screw-top jar;
shake well.
per serving 38g total fat (11.1g saturated fat);
2270kJ (543 cal); 13.1g carbohydrate;
35.2g protein; 5.3g fibre

Couscous, carrot and pistachio pilaf

preparation time 15 minutes
cooking time 10 minutes
serves 4

2 cups (500ml) water
2 cups (400g) couscous
1 small red onion (100g), chopped finely
1 tablespoon olive oil
2 large carrots (360g), sliced thinly
1 cup (120g) stuffed green olives, halved
½ cup (70g) roasted unsalted pistachios,
    chopped coarsely
420g can chickpeas, rinsed, drained
1 cup loosely packed fresh coriander leaves
sumac dressing
⅓ cup (80ml) olive oil
½ cup (125ml) lemon juice
3 teaspoons sumac

1   Bring the water to a boil in medium saucepan.
Remove from heat; stir in couscous and onion.
Cover; stand about 5 minutes or until liquid is
absorbed, fluffing with fork occasionally.
2   Meanwhile, heat oil in large frying pan; cook
carrot, covered, about 3 minutes or until just tender.
Uncover; cook 3 minutes.
3   Make sumac dressing.
4   Combine couscous mixture with carrot, dressing
and remaining ingredients in large bowl.
sumac dressing Combine ingredients in screw-top
jar; shake well.
per serving 36.3g total fat (4.9g saturated fat);
3436kJ (822 cal); 95.9g carbohydrate;
22.4g protein; 11g fibre

Mixed bean, ham and bread salad

preparation time 10 minutes
cooking time 5 minutes
serves 4

200g green beans, trimmed, halved
1 small loaf turkish bread (160g)
200g piece ham, chopped coarsely
400g can borlotti beans, rinsed, drained
4 cornichons (60g), halved lengthways
⅓ cup (80ml) cream
1 tablespoon lemon juice
1 tablespoon wholegrain mustard
1 tablespoon finely chopped fresh tarragon

1 Preheat grill.
2 Boil, steam or microwave green beans until tender; drain. Rinse under cold water; drain.
3 Meanwhile, cut bread into 2cm cubes. Toast under grill until crisp.
4 Combine beans and bread with remaining ingredients in large bowl.

per serving 12.4g total fat (6.6g saturated fat); 1300kJ (311 cal); 27.5g carbohydrate; 18.9g protein; 7g fibre

BLT salad

preparation time 10 minutes
cooking time 15 minutes
serves 4

250g cherry tomatoes
cooking-oil spray
6 rashers rindless bacon (390g)
1 small french bread stick (150g)
180g bocconcini cheese, halved
1 large cos lettuce, leaves separated, torn
mustard mayonnaise
⅓ cup (100g) mayonnaise
2 teaspoons wholegrain mustard
¼ cup (60ml) lemon juice

1 Preheat grill. Make mustard mayonnaise.
2 Place tomatoes on oven tray; spray with oil.
Grill until softened slightly. Cover to keep warm.
3 Grill bacon until crisp. Chop coarsely.
4 Cut bread into 8 slices; toast under grill until
browned both sides.
5 Combine half the tomato, half the bacon, half
the cheese and lettuce in large bowl. Divide salad
among serving dishes; sprinkle with remaining
tomato, bacon and cheese. Serve salad with toast;
drizzle with mayonnaise.
mustard mayonnaise Combine ingredients in
smal bowl.
per serving 31.2g total fat (16.4g saturated fat);
2312kJ (553 cal); 31.1g carbohydrate;
33.9g protein; 7.1g fibre

Orange, beetroot and roast beef salad

preparation time 15 minutes
serves 4

2 medium oranges (480g)
400g shaved rare roast beef
850g can whole baby beetroot, drained, halved
150g baby rocket leaves
½ cup (125ml) buttermilk
¼ cup (75g) mayonnaise
1 tablespoon wholegrain mustard
100g blue cheese, crumbled

1 Segment oranges over large bowl; reserve
1 tablespoon juice separately.
2 Add beef, beetroot and rocket to bowl.
3 Whisk reserved juice with buttermilk, mayonnaise
and mustard in small bowl. Sprinkle cheese over
salad; drizzle with dressing.

per serving 19.9g total fat (8.4g saturated fat);
1860kJ (445 cal); 26.8g carbohydrate;
36.4g protein; 6.2g fibre

Salami, bocconcini and pasta salad

preparation time 10 minutes
cooking time 15 minutes
serves 6

500g mini penne pasta
½ cup (75g) seeded black olives, halved
250g cherry tomatoes, halved
180g bocconcini cheese, halved
100g spicy salami, chopped coarsely
1 cup firmly packed fresh basil leaves
red wine vinaigrette
⅓ cup (80ml) olive oil
¼ cup (60ml) red wine vinegar
2 teaspoons dijon mustard
1 clove garlic, crushed

1 Cook pasta in large saucepan of boiling water, uncovered, until just tender; drain. Rinse under cold water; drain.
2 Meanwhile, make red wine vinaigrette.
3 Combine pasta, vinaigrette and remaining ingredients in large bowl.
red wine vinaigrette Combine ingredients in screw-top jar; shake well.
per serving 24.1g total fat (4.9g saturated fat); 2274kJ (544 cal); 61g carbohydrate; 18.6g protein; 3.9g fibre

Smoked trout and potato salad

preparation time 5 minutes
cooking time 25 minutes
serves 4

750g baby new potatoes, halved
2 x 385g whole smoked trout
2 tablespoons lemon juice
1 tablespoon olive oil
1 teaspoon dijon mustard
1 small red onion (100g), sliced thinly
2 green onions, sliced thinly
2 tablespoons capers, rinsed, drained
1 tablespoon finely chopped fresh dill
4 large iceberg lettuce leaves

1 Boil, steam or microwave potato until tender; drain. Cook potato on heated oiled grill plate (or grill or barbecue) until browned both sides.
2 Meanwhile, discard skin and bones from fish; flake flesh into large bowl.
3 Combine juice, oil and mustard in screw-top jar; shake well.
4 Combine potato, dressing, onions, capers and dill in bowl with trout; divide salad among lettuce leaves.
per serving 16.6g total fat (1.9g saturated fat); 1404kJ (336 cal); 27.6g carbohydrate; 31.2g protein; 4.8g fibre

Smoked chicken, radicchio and basil leaf salad

preparation time 10 minutes
cooking time 5 minutes
serves 4

340g asparagus, trimmed, chopped coarsely
500g smoked chicken breast fillets, sliced thickly
2 medium radicchio (400g), trimmed, leaves torn
⅔ cup loosely packed fresh basil leaves
pesto dressing
2 teaspoons basil pesto
¼ cup (60ml) balsamic vinegar
¼ cup (60ml) olive oil

1 Boil, steam or microwave asparagus until tender; drain. Rinse under cold water; drain.
2 Meanwhile, make pesto dressing.
3 Combine asparagus, dressing and remaining ingredients in large bowl.
pesto dressing Combine ingredients in screw-top jar; shake well.
per serving 23.8g total fat (4.6g saturated fat); 1513kJ (362 cal); 2g carbohydrate; 33.8g protein; 3.2g fibre

Warm pasta, pea and ricotta salad

preparation time 10 minutes
cooking time 15 minutes
serves 4

375g orecchiette pasta
1½ cups (200g) frozen baby peas
½ cup coarsely chopped fresh mint
100g shaved ham, chopped coarsely
1 teaspoon finely grated lemon rind
200g ricotta cheese, crumbled
buttermilk aïoli
⅓ cup (100g) mayonnaise
2 tablespoons buttermilk
2 teaspoons lemon juice
1 clove garlic, crushed
1 teaspoon finely grated lemon rind

1 Cook pasta in large saucepan of boiling water, uncovered, until just tender; drain.
2 Boil, steam or microwave peas until tender; drain.
3 Meanwhile, make buttermilk aïoli.
4 Combine warm pasta, peas and remaining ingredients in large bowl. Serve salad sprinkled with cheese.
buttermilk aïoli Combine ingredients in small bowl.
per serving 16.2g total fat (5.2g saturated fat); 2328kJ (557 cal); 74.5g carbohydrate; 24.3g protein; 6.8g fibre

tip If you can't find orecchiette, replace it with penne, the quill-shaped pasta.

Radicchio, pumpkin and haloumi salad

preparation time 10 minutes
cooking time 20 minutes
serves 4

1kg piece pumpkin, cut into 12 wedges
180g haloumi cheese
¼ cup (60ml) lemon juice
2 tablespoons olive oil
1 tablespoon baby capers, rinsed, drained
1 medium radicchio (200g), trimmed,
    leaves separated
½ cup firmly packed fresh flat-leaf parsley leaves
¼ cup (50g) roasted pepitas

1 Boil, steam or microwave pumpkin until tender; drain.
2 Cut cheese horizontally into four slices, cut each slice into four triangles.
3 Cook pumpkin and cheese, in batches, on heated oiled grill plate (or grill or barbecue) until browned.
4 Meanwhile, combine juice, oil and capers in screw-top jar; shake well.
5 Combine radicchio in large bowl with dressing and parsley. Divide salad among serving plates; top with pumpkin, cheese and pepitas.
per serving 22g total fat (6.8g saturated fat); 1363kJ (326 cal); 15.2g carbohydrate; 14.8g protein; 5.2g fibre

Smoked chicken and craisin salad

preparation time 15 minutes
serves 4

2 teaspoons dijon mustard
¼ cup (60ml) apple cider vinegar
2 tablespoons olive oil
500g smoked chicken breast fillets,
    shredded coarsely
1 large green apple (200g), sliced thinly
1 cup (120g) roasted pecans
½ cup (65g) craisins
150g baby spinach leaves
1 cup loosely packed fresh parsley leaves

1 Combine mustard, vinegar and oil in screw-top jar; shake well.
2 Combine dressing with remaining ingredients in large bowl.
per serving 39.8g total fat (5.2g saturated fat); 2420kJ (579 cal); 17.7g carbohydrate; 35.5g protein; 5.9g fibre

Turkish lamb and yogurt salad

preparation time 15 minutes
cooking time 10 minutes
serves 4

600g lamb backstrap
2 tablespoons sumac
1 tablespoon olive oil
¼ cup (70g) yogurt
2 tablespoons lemon juice
250g cherry tomatoes, halved
2 lebanese cucumbers (260g),
    seeded, sliced thinly
½ cup loosely packed fresh
    flat-leaf parsley leaves
½ cup loosely packed fresh mint leaves
1 small red onion (100g), sliced thinly

1 Rub lamb with sumac. Heat oil in large frying pan; cook lamb, uncovered, until cooked as desired. Cover, stand 5 minutes; slice thinly.
2 Meanwhile, whisk yogurt and juice in small jug.
3 Combine lamb and remaining ingredients in large bowl with dressing.
per serving 10.8g total fat (3.4g saturated fat); 1062kJ (254 cal); 5.1g carbohydrate; 32.9g protein; 2.7g fibre

Pizza

kalamata olives

These popular olives take their name from the Greek city where the fruit is thought to have first been grown. Slightly almond-shaped, and a deep-purple to black in colour, kalamata olives have a rich, fruity flavour and are sometimes sold slit or slightly crushed, to absorb more of the red-wine brine in which they are traditionally marinated. The plump olives' inherent salty and juicy qualities make them ideal for use on a pizza: they enhance the taste of the other ingredients and don't shrivel dry in a hot pizza oven. Kalamatas go well with cheeses such as fetta, romano and provolone, mushrooms, and char-grilled capsicum, eggplant and artichokes – essentially, all the usual suspects on a perfect pizza.

parmesan cheese

Parmesan, the hard, grainy cow-milk cheese traditionally made in the northern Italian regions of Reggio Emilia and Parma, has been copied all over the world but never duplicated. Reggiano and grana, the two best-known imports, are aged, flaky and sharp. The cheese's scent is both fragrant and savoury, its taste almost nutty and delicately pungent, and a shard broken off and tossed into the mouth is strong, tingly and creamy at the same time. Grated or flaked on a pizza, over pasta or in a salad, parmesan adds just the right note to tie the dish's other ingredients, especially tomato, oregano, basil and chilli, into a finished delight... and a chunk eaten on its own with fruit isn't so bad, either.

hot sopressa

Hot sopressa, sometimes sold as chilli sopressa, is a northern-style Italian salami usually made from pork flavoured with chilli, pepper, clove, cinnamon, nutmeg, rosemary and garlic then lightly smoked. Polenta and sopressa, both from the Veneto region, of which Venice is the epicentre, are often served together, their respective flavours and textures being perfect foils for one another. Sopressa salami is superb, too, sliced thinly or cut into slivers and sprinkled over a pizza before it is baked; scatter baby rocket leaves and flaked pecorino over the hot pizza just before serving for a taste sensation. Sopressa and prawns, surprisingly perhaps, also conspire to make a fabulous pizza topping.

char-grilled red capsicum

A few hours spent in the kitchen on the weekend will go a long way towards simplifying an evening meal. Char-grill and peel several capsicums at one time then store the roasted sliced flesh, covered with olive oil in a tightly sealed glass jar, in your fridge, taking out only as much as you need for any given recipe. Roasted red capsicums are very different in taste from raw ones; the peeling away of the bitter skin and cooking the flesh releases their lusciously sweet flavour. One of the simplest but most delicious of all pizza toppings is some thinly sliced roasted red capsicum drizzled with extra virgin olive oil then given a scatter of sea salt, crushed garlic and grated smoked mozzarella.

Prawn and grilled capsicum pizza

preparation time 10 minutes
cooking time 20 minutes
serves 4

We used small (15cm diameter)
packaged pizza bases for this recipe.

720g uncooked medium king prawns
1 tablespoon olive oil
4 cloves garlic, crushed
2 fresh small red thai chillies, chopped finely
4 x 112g pizza bases
⅓ cup (90g) tomato paste
½ cup (50g) coarsely grated mozzarella cheese
270g jar char-grilled capsicum in oil, drained,
  chopped coarsely
¼ cup (20g) flaked parmesan cheese
⅓ cup loosely packed fresh basil leaves

1 Preheat oven to 220°C/200°C fan-forced. Oil
two oven trays.
2 Shell and devein prawns; combine with oil,
garlic and chilli in large bowl.
3 Cook prawn mixture in heated large frying pan
until prawns are changed in colour.
4 Spread bases with paste; top with mozzarella,
prawns and capsicum. Cook, uncovered, about
15 minutes. Sprinkle pizzas with parmesan and basil.
per serving 16.9g total fat (4.4g saturated fat);
2328kJ (557 cal); 62.6g carbohydrate;
35.1g protein; 5.7g fibre

Pizza caprese

preparation time 10 minutes
cooking time 15 minutes
serves 4

**We used large (25cm diameter)
packaged pizza bases for this recipe.**

2 x 335g pizza bases
½ cup (140g) tomato paste
4 large egg tomatoes (360g), sliced thinly
210g bocconcini cheese, halved
¼ cup finely shredded fresh basil

1 Preheat oven to 220°C/200°C fan-forced. Oil
two oven trays.
2 Spread bases with paste; top with tomato and
cheese. Cook, uncovered, about 15 minutes.
Sprinkle pizzas with basil.

per serving 14.6g total fat (6.1g saturated fat);
2658kJ (636 cal); 94.5g carbohydrate;
26.1g protein; 9g fibre

Tex-Mex pizza

preparation time 10 minutes
cooking time 15 minutes
serves 4

We used small (15cm diameter) packaged pizza
bases for this recipe.
A Mexican staple, frijoles refritos (refried beans) are
sold canned in supermarkets. You will also find spicy
tomato salsa in supermarkets.

4 x 112g pizza bases
¾ cup (180g) refried beans
½ cup (130g) spicy tomato salsa
½ small red onion (50g), sliced thinly
½ cup (50g) coarsely grated pizza cheese
1 medium avocado (250g), sliced thinly
2 tablespoons fresh coriander leaves

1 Preheat oven to 220°C/200°C fan-forced. Oil
two oven trays.
2 Spread bases with beans; top with salsa and
onion, sprinkle with cheese. Cook, uncovered, about
15 minutes. Top pizzas with avocado and coriander.
per serving 17.5g total fat (4.6g saturated fat);
2157kJ (516 cal); 67.5g carbohydrate;
18g protein; 7.9g fibre

Ham, sage and fontina pizza

preparation time 10 minutes
cooking time 10 minutes
serves 4

We used large (25cm diameter) packaged pizza
bases for this recipe.
Fontina is an Italian cow-milk cheese that has a
smooth but firm texture and a mild, nutty flavour. It
is an ideal melting or grilling cheese, and is often
used in the Italian version of fondue. You could use
mozzarella or taleggio as a substitute.

2 x 335g pizza bases
1 tablespoon olive oil
2 cloves garlic, crushed
2 tablespoons finely chopped fresh sage
100g thinly sliced ham
200g fontina cheese, sliced thinly

1 Preheat oven to 220°C/200°C fan-forced. Oil
two oven trays.
2 Spread bases with combined oil, garlic and
sage; top with ham and cheese. Cook, uncovered,
about 10 minutes.
per serving 26.8g total fat (11.3g saturated fat);
3110kJ (744 cal); 89g carbohydrate;
33g protein; 6.5g fibre

Roasted eggplant and chorizo pizza

preparation time 10 minutes
cooking time 15 minutes
serves 4

**We used small (15cm diameter)
packaged pizza bases for this recipe.**

4 x 112g pizza bases
⅓ cup (90g) sun-dried tomato pesto
320g jar char-grilled eggplant in oil,
    drained, chopped coarsely
½ cup (75g) seeded kalamata olives
1 chorizo sausage (170g), sliced thinly
½ cup (50g) coarsely grated pizza cheese
¼ cup loosely packed fresh oregano leaves

1 Preheat oven to 220°C/200°C fan-forced. Oil
two oven trays.
2 Spread bases with pesto; top with eggplant,
olives and chorizo, sprinkle with cheese. Cook,
uncovered, about 15 minutes. Sprinkle pizzas
with oregano.

per serving 40.7g total fat (16.3g saturated fat);
3089kJ (739 cal); 66.2g carbohydrate;
25g protein; 5.1g fibre

Chicken, artichoke and fetta pizza

preparation time 10 minutes
cooking time 15 minutes
serves 4

We used large (25cm diameter) packaged pizza bases for this recipe.
You will need to purchase half a large barbecued chicken weighing approximately 450g to get the amount of shredded meat required for this recipe.

2 x 335g pizza bases
2 tablespoons olive oil
1 clove garlic, crushed
2 cups (320g) shredded cooked chicken
340g jar marinated artichoke hearts in oil, drained, chopped coarsely
180g fetta cheese, crumbled
⅓ cup finely shredded fresh mint
2 teaspoons finely grated lemon rind

1 Preheat oven to 220°C/200°C fan-forced. Oil two oven trays.
2 Spread bases with combined oil and garlic; top with chicken, artichoke and cheese. Cook, uncovered, about 15 minutes. Sprinkle pizzas with mint and rind.

per serving 32.3g total fat (10.8g saturated fat); 3532kJ (845 cal); 89.9g carbohydrate; 44g protein; 8.3g fibre

Pepperoni pizza

preparation time 10 minutes
cooking time 15 minutes
serves 4

We used large (25cm diameter)
packaged pizza bases for this recipe.

2 x 335g pizza bases
½ cup (140g) tomato paste
125g pepperoni, sliced thinly
4 slices (170g) roasted red capsicum,
    sliced thickly
¼ cup (40g) seeded kalamata olives
1 cup (80g) flaked parmesan cheese
2 tablespoons fresh oregano leaves

1 Preheat oven to 220°C/200°C fan-forced. Oil
two oven trays.
2 Spread bases with paste; top with pepperoni,
capsicum and olives, sprinkle with cheese. Cook,
uncovered, about 15 minutes. Sprinkle pizzas
with oregano.
per serving 24.4g total fat (9g saturated fat);
3156kJ (755 cal); 97g carbohydrate;
31.9g protein; 8.3g fibre

Smoked cheese and sopressa pizza

preparation time 10 minutes
cooking time 15 minutes
serves 4

**We used large (25cm diameter)
packaged pizza bases for this recipe.**

2 x 335g pizza bases
½ cup (140g) tomato paste
100g hot sopressa, sliced thinly
1 cup (150g) semi-dried tomatoes, drained,
    chopped coarsely
100g smoked cheese, flaked
50g baby rocket leaves

1 Preheat oven to 220°C/200°C fan-forced. Oil
two oven trays.
2 Spread bases with paste; top with sopressa
and tomato. Cook, uncovered, about 15 minutes.
Top pizzas with cheese and rocket.
per serving 24.6g total fat (5.4g saturated fat);
3352kJ (802 cal); 106.3g carbohydrate;
31.5g protein; 13.3g fibre

Dessert

sponge-finger biscuits

Savoiardi, from the Piedmont region (once known as the Duchy of Savoy, hence the biscuit's name), is what the Italians call the sponge-finger biscuit, a ready-to-use staple that can be kept in your pantry for a quick midweek dessert. Be certain the ones you use are still crunchy and crisp; if soft, they've passed their use-by-date. Their hardened cell structure is not unlike that of a sponge, which makes them excellent in absorbing liquids – a culinary requisite when making a quick parfait, tiramisu, trifle or charlotte. Try crushing them instead of ordinary biscuits for a hedgehog slice; they make a good partner for zabaglione and, naturally enough, are fine eaten just as they come.

frozen mixed berries

The answer to a cook's prayers: available year round, they are never subject to seasonal price or quality fluctuations. Frozen mixed berries should be found in the freezer of every cook who wants to get a quick dessert on the table on a weeknight. They don't need to be thawed if going into a crumble, summer pudding or sweet sauce; in fact, it's better if they're not, to help keep the juice from "bleeding" into the dessert's other ingredients. They are great folded into softened vanilla ice cream, which is then re-frozen, or combined with ready-made custard and jam roll for a practically instant trifle. Kids love to "cook" with them, too: they can be used to make the best ice blocks and smoothies imaginable.

mascarpone

People are often confused about whether to regard mascarpone as a cheese or a thick cream: we just think of it as delicious. A fresh triple-cream cheese from Italy's Lombardy region, it probably first became known to us when tiramisu was the dessert du jour of the mid-'80s. Made from cultured cows' milk, its texture can be compared to that of softened butter. It can be spread over a cake to ice it or onto pieces of firm fresh fruit. Like most wonderfully indulgent foods, there is no real substitute for mascarpone, but it can certainly serve to replace vanilla ice-cream, pouring cream or triple cream on top of a warm sticky date pudding or alongside a bowl of fresh or poached seasonal fruit.

hazelnuts

Also known as filberts, this plump, grape-size nut has an inedible bitter brown skin that has to be removed before the nuts can be used. Toast the nuts briefly in a frying pan or the oven, stirring constantly to ensure they don't burn. Cool then rub the warm nuts together vigorously in a tea towel; discard the skins. The marriage between hazelnuts and chocolate and coffee, together or individually, in a recipe produces a match made in heaven, and hazelnut meal results in a terrific friand. Crush the roasted nuts and use them in a butterscotch sauce, a dessert crepe or stirred through some mascarpone when you dollop it over fruit. And never, ever, pass on the offer of hazelnut gelato.

Walnut and ricotta-stuffed figs

preparation time 10 minutes
cooking time 10 minutes
serves 4

8 medium figs (480g)
¼ cup (25g) roasted walnuts, chopped coarsely
½ cup (120g) ricotta cheese
1 tablespoon caster sugar
⅓ cup (80ml) cream
30g butter
⅓ cup (75g) firmly packed brown sugar

1 Preheat oven to 200°C/180°C fan-forced.
2 Cut figs, from the top, into quarters, being careful not to cut all the way through; open slightly. Place on oven tray.
3 Combine nuts, cheese and sugar in small bowl; divide nut mixture among figs. Cook, uncovered, about 10 minutes or until figs are heated through.
4 Meanwhile, combine remaining ingredients in small saucepan; stir over heat until sugar dissolves. Simmer, uncovered, 3 minutes.
5 Place two figs in each serving dish; drizzle with caramel sauce.

per serving 22.8g total fat (12.2g saturated fat); 1526kJ (365 cal); 32.6g carbohydrate; 6g protein; 3.1g fibre

Balsamic strawberries with mascarpone

preparation time 5 minutes
(plus refrigeration time)
serves 4

500g strawberries, halved
¼ cup (55g) caster sugar
2 tablespoons balsamic vinegar
1 cup (250g) mascarpone cheese
1 tablespoon icing sugar
1 teaspoon vanilla extract
¼ cup coarsely chopped fresh mint

1 Combine strawberries, sugar and vinegar in medium bowl, cover; refrigerate 20 minutes.
2 Meanwhile, combine mascarpone, icing sugar and extract in small bowl.
3 Stir mint into strawberry mixture; divide among serving dishes. Serve with mascarpone.

per serving 29.8g total fat (20.3g saturated fat); 1572kJ (376 cal); 21.2g carbohydrate; 5.2g protein; 3g fibre

Passionfruit and banana sundae

preparation time 5 minutes
cooking time 10 minutes
serves 4

**You need six passionfruit for this recipe.
Mini pavlova shells are sold in all supermarkets.**

300ml thickened cream
2 tablespoons lemon-flavoured spread
50g mini pavlova shells, chopped coarsely
½ cup (125ml) passionfruit pulp
4 small bananas (520g), chopped coarsely

1 Beat cream and spread in small bowl with electric mixer until soft peaks form.
2 Layer lemon cream, pavlova pieces, passionfruit and banana among serving glasses.
per serving 28.6g total fat (18.5g saturated fat); 1839kJ (440 cal); 38.9g carbohydrate; 4.4g protein; 6.3g fibre

Berry, coconut and yogurt parfaits

preparation time 10 minutes
serves 6

**This dessert can be made several hours in
advance; store, covered, in the refrigerator.**

tip Do not defrost berries before blending.

1 cup (150g) frozen mixed berries
1 tablespoon caster sugar
1 tablespoon coconut-flavoured liqueur
1 cup (250ml) raspberry and cranberry juice
12 sponge-finger biscuits (140g)
500g vanilla yogurt
2 tablespoons flaked coconut, toasted

1 Blend or process berries, sugar, liqueur and
¼ cup of juice until smooth.
2 Dip biscuits in remaining juice; divide among
six 1½-cup (375ml) serving glasses.
3 Divide half the yogurt among glasses; top with
half the berry mixture. Repeat layering with remaining
yogurt and berry mixture. Sprinkle with coconut.
per serving 5.2g total fat (3.3g saturated fat); 882kJ
(211 cal); 31.5g carbohydrate; 6.5g protein; 1.1g fibre

Berry hazelnut crumbles

preparation time 10 minutes
cooking time 20 minutes
serves 4

2 cups (300g) frozen mixed berries
1 tablespoon lemon juice
2 tablespoons brown sugar
½ cup (60g) finely chopped roasted hazelnuts
2 tablespoons plain flour
20g cold butter
¼ cup (20g) rolled oats

1 Preheat oven to 220°C/200°C fan-forced. Grease four shallow ¾-cup (180ml) ovenproof dishes; place on oven tray.
2 Combine berries, juice, half the sugar and half the nuts in medium bowl; divide mixture among dishes.
3 Blend or process remaining sugar and nuts with flour and butter until ingredients come together; stir in oats. Sprinkle over berry mixture.
4 Bake, uncovered, about 20 minutes or until browned lightly.
per serving 14.6g total fat (3.2g saturated fat); 915kJ (219 cal); 16.8g carbohydrate; 4.8g protein; 3.9g fibre

 goes well with custard.

Lemon and mixed berry self-saucing pudding

preparation time 15 minutes
cooking time 15 minutes
serves 4

¾ cup (110g) self-raising flour
½ cup (110g) caster sugar
½ cup (125ml) skim milk
1 tablespoon finely grated lemon rind
30g unsalted butter, melted
⅓ cup (55g) icing sugar
⅔ cup (160ml) boiling water
mixed berry sauce
1 cup (150g) frozen mixed berries
1 tablespoon caster sugar
1 tablespoon water

1 Grease four deep 1¼-cup (310ml) microwave-proof dishes.
2 Make mixed berry sauce.
3 Sift flour into medium bowl. Add sugar, milk, rind and butter; whisk until batter is smooth.
4 Divide berry sauce among dishes then top with batter; dust with sifted icing sugar. Pour hot water over puddings. Microwave, uncovered, on MEDIUM (55%) about 10 minutes.
mixed berry sauce Combine ingredients in small saucepan; bring to a boil. Boil, uncovered, 1 minute. Remove from heat.

per serving 6.6g total fat (4.2g saturated fat); 1505kJ (360 cal); 68.4g carbohydrate; 4.8g protein; 2g fibre

Hazelnut tiramisu

preparation time 20 minutes
serves 6

1 tablespoon instant coffee granules
2 tablespoons caster sugar
⅔ cup (160ml) boiling water
⅓ cup (80ml) hazelnut-flavoured liqueur
½ cup (125ml) cream
1 cup (250g) mascarpone cheese
12 sponge-finger biscuits (140g)
¼ cup (25g) coarsely grated dark chocolate
½ cup (70g) coarsely chopped roasted hazelnuts

1 Dissolve coffee and half the sugar in the water in medium heatproof bowl. Stir in liqueur; cool.
2 Meanwhile, beat cream and remaining sugar in small bowl with electric mixer until soft peaks form; fold in mascarpone.
3 Dip biscuits, one at a time, in coffee mixture; place in single layer in shallow 2-litre (8-cup) serving dish. Pour any remaining coffee mixture over biscuits. Spread cream mixture over biscuits; sprinkle with combined chocolate and nuts. Refrigerate until required.

per serving 40.5g total fat (22.2g saturated fat); 2153kJ (515 cal); 24.5g carbohydrate; 7g protein; 2g fibre

Butterscotch nougat bananas

preparation time 10 minutes
cooking time 5 minutes
serves 4

40g butter
¼ cup (55g) firmly packed brown sugar
4 small bananas (520g), cut into thirds
½ cup (125ml) thickened cream
2 tablespoons vanilla yogurt
50g nougat, chopped finely
¼ cup (35g) slivered almonds, roasted

1 Melt butter with sugar in large frying pan. Add bananas; cook, over low heat, about 5 minutes, turning occasionally, until caramelised.
2 Meanwhile, beat cream in small bowl with electric mixer until soft peaks form; fold in yogurt and nougat.
3 Serve bananas topped with nougat cream and sprinkled with nuts.

per serving 26.2g total fat (13.7g saturated fat); 1793kJ (429 cal); 42.4g carbohydrate; 5.1g protein; 2.8g fibre

Mango galettes with coconut cream

preparation time 10 minutes
cooking time 15 minutes
serves 4

1 sheet puff pastry, quartered
20g butter, melted
2 firm medium mangoes (860g), halved,
   sliced thinly
1 tablespoon brown sugar
⅔ cup (160ml) thickened cream, whipped
2 teaspoons coconut-flavoured liqueur
⅓ cup (15g) flaked coconut, toasted

1 Preheat oven to 200°C/180°C fan-forced.
Grease oven tray; line with baking paper.
2 Place pastry squares on oven tray, prick with
fork; brush with half the melted butter. Divide
mango among pastry squares, leaving 2cm border.
Sprinkle sugar over galettes; drizzle with remaining
butter. Bake, uncovered, about 15 minutes.
3 Meanwhile, combine remaining ingredients in
small bowl. Serve galettes with coconut cream.
per serving 31.2g total fat (19.7g saturated fat);
1969kJ (471 cal); 40.1g carbohydrate;
5g protein; 3.4g fibre

Pears with choc-mint sauce

preparation time 5 minutes
cooking time 5 minutes
serves 4

200g peppermint cream dark chocolate,
    chopped coarsely
¼ cup (60ml) cream
825g can pear halves in natural juice, drained
1 litre vanilla ice-cream
4 (60g) mint slice biscuits, chopped finely

1 Melt chocolate with cream in medium
heatproof bowl set over medium saucepan
of simmering water.
2 Divide pears among serving dishes; top
with ice-cream, drizzle with sauce then sprinkle
with biscuits.
per serving 39.9g total fat (25.2g saturated fat);
2976kJ (712 cal); 77.9g carbohydrate;
9.3g protein; 2.7g fibre

Glossary

BABA GHANOUSH a favourite on Middle-Eastern tables, this dip is similar to another Middle-Eastern staple, hummus, but replaces chickpeas with roasted eggplant.

BABY CORN pale-yellow cobs of corn that are harvested while young and tender; can be eaten raw or cooked.

BEAN SPROUTS also known as bean shoots; tender new growths of beans and seeds germinated for consumption as sprouts. Most readily available are mung bean, soy bean, alfalfa and snow pea sprouts.

BEANS

borlotti also known as roman beans or pink beans; can be eaten fresh or dried. Interchangeable with pinto beans because of the similarity in appearance – both are pale pink or beige with dark red streaks.

white in this book, some recipes may simply call for "white beans", a generic term we use for canned or dried cannellini, haricot, navy or great northern beans.

BEEF EYE-FILLET tenderloin fillet with a fine texture; is extremely tender and expensive.

BLACK OLIVE TAPENADE a thick paste made from black olives, capers, anchovies, olive oil and lemon juice.

BREADCRUMBS

fresh usually white bread that is processed into crumbs.

packaged prepared fine-textured but crunchy white breadcrumbs.

stale crumbs made by blending or processing 1- or 2-day-old bread.

BROCCOLINI a cross between broccoli and chinese kale; long asparagus-like stems with a long loose floret, both completely edible. Resembles broccoli in look but is milder and sweeter in taste.

BUTTERMILK sold in the dairy section in supermarkets. Originally the term given to the slightly sour liquid left after butter was churned from cream, today it is commercially made similarly to yogurt.

CAPSICUM also known as bell pepper or pepper. Seeds and membranes should be discarded before use.

CHEESE

blue mould-treated cheeses mottled with blue veining. Varieties include firm and crumbly stilton types and mild, creamy brie-like cheeses.

bocconcini the term used for walnut-sized baby mozzarella; a delicate, semi-soft, white cheese. *Cherry bocconcini* are smaller than regular mozzarella. Both spoil rapidly so must be kept, under refrigeration, in brine, for no more than 2 days.

fetta a crumbly goat- or sheep-milk cheese with a sharp salty taste.

haloumi a firm, cream-coloured sheep-milk cheese matured in brine. Somewhat like a minty, salty fetta in flavour; can be grilled or fried, briefly, without breaking down.

mozzarella soft, spun-curd cheese generally made from cow milk; has a low melting point and elastic properties when heated. Is used for texture rather than flavour.

pizza commercial blend of varying proportions of processed grated mozzarella, cheddar and parmesan.

ricotta a soft, sweet, moist, white cow-milk cheese with a low fat content and a slightly grainy texture. The name roughly translates as "cooked again" and refers to ricotta's manufacture from a whey that is itself a by-product of other cheese making.

smoked creamy in colour and smoky in flavour; available from specialist cheese stores and supermarkets.

CHINESE BARBECUED DUCK traditionally cooked in special ovens, it has a sweet-sticky coating made from soy sauce, five-spice, sherry and hoisin sauce. Available from Asian food stores and specialty barbecue shops.

CHINESE COOKING WINE also known as hao hsing or chinese rice wine; made from fermented rice, wheat, sugar and salt with a 13.5 per cent alcohol content. Found in Asian food shops; if you can't find it, replace with mirin or sherry.

CHORIZO SAUSAGE of Spanish origin; made of coarsely ground pork and highly seasoned with garlic and chilli.

CHOY SUM also known as pakaukeo or flowering cabbage, a member of the buk choy family; easy to identify with its long stems, light green leaves and yellow flowers. Stems and leaves are both edible, steamed or stir-fried.

COCONUT

cream obtained commercially from the first pressing of the coconut flesh alone, without the addition of water. Available in cans and cartons at most supermarkets.

flaked dried flaked coconut flesh.

flavoured-liqueur we used Malibu.

milk not the liquid found inside the fruit (known as coconut water), but the diluted liquid (less rich) from the second pressing of the white flesh of a mature coconut. Available in cans and cartons at most supermarkets.

CORIANDER also known as cilantro or chinese parsley; bright-green-leafed herb with a pungent flavour. The stems and roots of coriander are also used in Thai cooking; wash well before chopping.

CORNICHON French for gherkin; a very small variety of pickled cucumber.

COS LETTUCE also known as romaine lettuce; the lettuce traditionally used in Caesar salad.

COUSCOUS a fine, grain-like cereal product from North Africa; made from semolina.

CURRY PASTES

green hottest of the traditional thai pastes; ingredients include green chilli, garlic, shallot, lemon grass, salt, galangal, shrimp paste, kaffir lime peel, coriander seed, pepper, cumin and turmeric. It is hotter than the milder thai red curry paste.

tandoori consists of garlic, ginger, tamarind, coriander, chilli and spices.

DIJON MUSTARD a pale brown, distinctively flavoured, fairly mild french mustard.

FLOUR, PLAIN also known as all-purpose; unbleached wheat flour is the best for baking: the gluten content ensures a strong dough, which produces a light result.

GAI LAN also known as gai larn, chinese broccoli and chinese kale; a green vegetable appreciated more for its stems than its coarse leaves.

KAFFIR LIME LEAVES also known as bai magrood; look like two glossy dark green leaves joined end to end, forming a rounded hourglass shape. Sold fresh, dried or frozen, the dried leaves are less potent so double the number if using them as a substitute for fresh; a strip of fresh lime peel may be substituted for each kaffir lime leaf.

HAZELNUT-FLAVOURED LIQUEUR we used Frangelico.

KUMARA Polynesian name of an orange-fleshed sweet potato often confused with yam.

LAMB BACKSTRAP also known as eye of loin; the larger fillet from a row of loin chops or cutlets. Tender and best cooked rapidly.

LEMON-FLAVOURED SPREAD commercially made lemon curd (a smooth spread, usually made from lemons, butter and eggs).

MAPLE SYRUP distilled from the sap of sugar maple trees. Maple-flavoured syrup or pancake syrup is not an adequate substitute for the real thing.

MINCE MEAT also known as ground meat as in beef, veal, lamb, pork and chicken.

MINT SLICE BISCUITS a chocolate biscuit topped with mint-flavoured cream, then coated in dark chocolate.

NOODLES
hokkien also known as stir-fry noodles. Fresh wheat flour noodles resembling thick, yellow-brown spaghetti; only require heating, not cooking.
soba thin Japanese noodles made from a mix of buckwheat flour and wheat flour; available fresh or dried.

OIL
peanut pressed from ground peanuts; has a high smoke point (capacity to handle high heat without burning).
sesame produced from roasted crushed sesame seeds; a flavouring rather than a cooking medium.

PAPRIKA ground dried red capsicum; sold in sweet, smoked or hot flavours.

PEAS
snow also called mange tout (eat all); a variety of garden pea, eaten pod and all (although you may need to string them).
sugar snap also known as honey snap peas; fresh small pea that can be eaten whole, pod and all.

PEPITAS pale green kernels of dried pumpkin seeds; they can be bought plain or salted.

PEPPERMINT CREAM DARK CHOCOLATE dark chocolate filled with peppermint-flavoured cream.

PEPPERONI spicy salami made of beef, pork and often veal.

PROSCIUTTO an unsmoked Italian ham that is salted, air-cured and aged. It is usually eaten uncooked.

RICE, WHITE LONG-GRAIN elongated grains that remain separate when cooked; a popular steaming rice.

ROCKET also known as arugula, rugula and rucola; peppery green leaf eaten raw in salads or used in cooking. *Baby rocket leaves* are smaller and less peppery.

ROLLED OATS flattened oat grain rolled into flakes and traditionally used for porridge. Instant oats are also available, but use traditional oats for baking.

SAMBAL OELEK (also sambal ulek or olek); a salty paste made from ground chillies, garlic and vinegar.

SAUCES
black bean a Chinese sauce made from fermented soy beans, spices, water and wheat flour.
char siu also known as chinese barbecue sauce. It is a paste-like ingredient that is dark-red-brown in colour and has a sweet and spicy flavour. Made with fermented soy beans, honey and various spices.
fish made from pulverised salted fermented fish (anchovies). Has a pungent smell and strong taste.
kecap manis a dark, thick sweet soy sauce with molasses or palm sugar added when brewed.
light soy fairly thin in consistency and, while paler than the others, is the saltiest tasting; used in dishes in which the natural colour of the ingredients is to be maintained. Not to be confused with salt-reduced or low-sodium soy sauces.
oyster made from oysters and their brine, cooked with salt and soy sauce, and thickened with starches.
plum a thick, sweet and sour dipping sauce made from plums, vinegar, sugar, chillies and spices.
sweet chilli the comparatively mild Thai sauce made from red chillies, sugar, garlic and vinegar.
teriyaki either commercially bottled or home-made, this Japanese sauce, made from soy sauce, mirin, sugar, ginger and other spices, imparts a distinctive glaze when brushed over grilled meat or poultry. Teriyaki actually translates as lustrous (teri) grilled (yaki) food.

SLIVERED ALMONDS small almond pieces cut lengthways.

SOPRESSA a semi-hard pork salami typically flavoured with pepper, cloves, cinnamon, nutmeg, rosemary and garlic; has a delicate, slightly sweet, taste.

SUGAR
brown a soft, finely granulated sugar with molasses for its characteristic colour and flavour.
caster also known as superfine or finely granulated table sugar.
icing also known as confectioners' sugar or powdered sugar; pulverised granulated sugar crushed together with a small amount of cornflour.
palm also known as jaggery or gula melaka; made from the sap of the sugar palm tree. Light- to dark-brown in colour and usually sold in rock-hard cakes. Substitute dark brown sugar if you can't find palm sugar.

THAI BASIL also known as horapa; is different from holy basil and sweet basil in both look and taste, having smaller leaves and purplish stems. It has a slight licorice or aniseed taste.

TOMATOES
cherry also known as tiny tim or tom thumb tomatoes; small and round.
egg also called plum or roma; these are smallish, oval-shaped tomatoes.

VANILLA EXTRACT obtained from vanilla beans infused in water; a non-alcoholic version of essence.

VIETNAMESE MINT not a mint at all, but a pungent and peppery narrow-leafed member of the buckwheat family. It is a common ingredient in Thai recipes.

VINEGAR
apple cider made from fermented apples. Available from supermarkets and health food stores.
balsamic originally from Modena, Italy, there are now many balsamic vinegars on the market ranging in pungency and quality depending on how, and how long, they have been aged. Quality can be determined up to a point by price; use the most expensive sparingly.
red wine made from red wine.

WATERCRESS one of the cress family, a large group of peppery greens. Highly perishable, so must be used as soon as possible after purchase.

WOMBOK also known as chinese cabbage; elongated with pale green crinkly leaves, is the most commonly used cabbage in South-East Asia.

ZUCCHINI also called courgette. A member of the squash family, having edible flowers.

Conversion Chart

measures

One Australian metric measuring cup holds approximately 250ml; one Australian metric tablespoon holds 20ml; one Australian metric teaspoon holds 5ml.

The difference between one country's measuring cups and another's is within a two- or three-teaspoon variance, and will not affect your cooking results. North America, New Zealand and the United Kingdom use a 15ml tablespoon.

All cup and spoon measurements are level. The most accurate way of measuring dry ingredients is to weigh them. When measuring liquids, use a clear glass or plastic jug with the metric markings.

We use large eggs with an average weight of 60g.

dry measures

metric	imperial
15g	½oz
30g	1oz
60g	2oz
90g	3oz
125g	4oz (¼lb)
155g	5oz
185g	6oz
220g	7oz
250g	8oz (½lb)
280g	9oz
315g	10oz
345g	11oz
375g	12oz (¾lb)
410g	13oz
440g	14oz
470g	15oz
500g	16oz (1lb)
750g	24oz (1½lb)
1kg	32oz (2lb)

liquid measures

metric	imperial
30ml	1 fluid oz
60ml	2 fluid oz
100ml	3 fluid oz
125ml	4 fluid oz
150ml	5 fluid oz (¼ pint/1 gill)
190ml	6 fluid oz
250ml	8 fluid oz
300ml	10 fluid oz (½ pint)
500ml	16 fluid oz
600ml	20 fluid oz (1 pint)
1000ml (1 litre)	1¾ pints

length measures

metric	imperial
3mm	⅛in
6mm	¼in
1cm	½in
2cm	¾in
2.5cm	1in
5cm	2in
6cm	2½in
8cm	3in
10cm	4in
13cm	5in
15cm	6in
18cm	7in
20cm	8in
23cm	9in
25cm	10in
28cm	11in
30cm	12in (1ft)

oven temperatures

These oven temperatures are only a guide for conventional ovens. For fan-forced ovens, check the manufacturer's manual.

	°C (Celsius)	°F (Fahrenheit)	Gas Mark
Very slow	120	250	½
Slow	150	275-300	1-2
Moderately slow	160	325	3
Moderate	180	350-375	4-5
Moderately hot	200	400	6
Hot	220	425-450	7-8
Very hot	240	475	9

Index

If you like this cookbook, you'll love these...

These are just a small selection of titles available in *The Australian Women's Weekly* range on sale at selected newsagents, supermarkets or online at www.acpbooks.com.au

also available in bookstores...

TEST KITCHEN
Food director Pamela Clark
Food editor Karen Hammial
Assistant food editor Sarah Schwikkard
Test Kitchen manager Cathie Lonnie
Senior home economist Elizabeth Macri
Home economists Nancy Duran, Belinda Farlow,
Miranda Farr, Nicole Jennings, Angela Muscat,
Rebecca Squadrito, Jacqui Storum, Kellie-Marie Thomas
Nutritional information Belinda Farlow

ACP BOOKS
Editorial director Susan Tomnay
Creative director & designer Hieu Chi Nguyen
Senior editor Wendy Bryant

Director of sales Brian Cearnes
Marketing manager Bridget Cody
Business analyst Ashley Davies

Chief executive officer Ian Law
Group publisher Pat Ingram
General manager Christine Whiston
Editorial director (WW) Deborah Thomas

RIGHTS ENQUIRIES
Laura Bamford Director ACP Books
lbamford@acpuk.com

Produced by ACP Books, Sydney.
Printed by Dai Nippon, c/o Samhwa Printing Co., Ltd,
237-10 Kuro-Dong, Kuro-Ku, Seoul, Korea.
Published by ACP Books, a division of
ACP Magazines Ltd, 54 Park St, Sydney;
GPO Box 4088, Sydney, NSW 2001.
phone (02) 9282 8618 fax (02) 9267 9438.
acpbooks@acpmagazines.com.au
www.acpbooks.com.au
To order books, phone 136 116 (within Australia).
Send recipe enquiries to:
recipeenquiries@acpmagazines.com.au

Australia Distributed by Network Services,
phone +61 2 9282 8777 fax +61 2 9264 3278
networkweb@networkservicescompany.com.au
United Kingdom Distributed by Australian Consolidated Press (UK),
phone (01604) 642 200 fax (01604) 642 300
books@acpuk.com
New Zealand Distributed by Netlink
Distribution Company,
phone (9) 366 9966 ask@ndc.co.nz
South Africa Distributed by PSD Promotions,
phone (27 11) 392 6065/6/7
fax (27 11) 392 6079/80
orders@psdprom.co.za

Clark, Pamela.
After work fast:
the Australian women's weekly.
Includes index.
ISBN 978-1-86396-580-4.
1. Quick and easy cookery.
I. Title. II Title: Australian women's weekly
641.555
© ACP Magazines Ltd 2007
ABN 18 053 273 546